TEN STEPS TO A FEDERAL JOB®

JOBSEEKER'S GUIDE

9TH EDITION

HOW TO LAND GOVERNMENT JOBS FOR MILITARY AND SPOUSES

KATHRYN TROUTMAN

Resume Place, Inc.
Federal Career Publishers

P.O. Box 21275, Catonsville, MD 21228 | Phone: 888-480-8265
Website: *www.resume-place.com* | Email: *resume@resume-place.com*

Printed in the United States of America
Jobseeker's Guide, 9th Edition - ISBN-13: 978-1-7334076-3-2
Updated December 2021

Attention Transition Counselors, Veterans' Representatives, Workforce Counselors, Career Counselors: The *Jobseeker's Guide* is a training program "handout" to support the Ten Steps to a Federal Job® workshops and PowerPoint program, which is taught at military bases, universities, one-stops, and DOD agencies worldwide. To be licensed to teach the Ten Steps to a Federal Job® curriculum as a Certified Federal Job Search Trainer® or Certified Federal Career Coach®, go to *www.resume-place.com* for information on our train-the-trainer program. Since the program was developed in 2002, more than 4,000 individuals have been licensed to teach Ten Steps to a Federal Job® with this guide as the handout.

AUTHOR'S NOTES

Sample resumes are real but fictionalized. All Federal applicants have given permission for their resumes to be used as samples for this publication. Privacy policy is strictly enforced.

Federal Resume Samples: *Veterans:* **Cedrick Sauls, Justus Casino, Julia Kelly, Jonathan Calderon;** *Military Spouses (Derived Preference):* **Maxine Mendez and Goodnite Hay;** *State of VA Veterans Representative:* **Mary Ann Bowersock;** *Retired US Army ACS Employment Readiness Program Manager:* **Mike Kozlowski;** *Administrative Officer, DEA, San Diego Field Division:* **Greg Hall.**

PUBLICATION TEAM

Cover and Interior Page Design: Brian Moore
Illustrator: Russell Yerkes
Developmental Editing: Paulina Chen
Copyediting/Proofreading: Robin Quinn
Federal Staffing, Veterans' Preference, and Schedule A SMEs: Charles Clark (USAF Retired), and Ligaya Fernandez
Updates on Agency List and Chapters: John Gagnon, Ph.D., J.D.
Program S Contributor: Bobbi Rossiter
Curriculum Design: Emily Troutman, MPP

TABLE OF CONTENTS

INTRODUCTION

WRITING & GETTING YOURSELF BEST QUALIFIED, REFERRED, INTERVIEWED & HIRED!

This book will teach you the Ten Steps to a Federal Job® and how to write your Federal resume correctly using the Outline Format, which is preferred by HR specialists. The next warm-up activity will introduce you to the Outline Format beginning with "How Many Hats Do You Wear at Work?" These "hats" are also keywords and transferrable skills. This is the beginning of Federal Resume Writing!

ACTIVITY: How Many Hats Do You Wear at Work?

Everyone wears different "hats" at work. You can also think about your skills or leadership in different disciplines or programs. These hats and disciplines are KEYWORDS for your Federal resume. Make a list of five to seven hats you wear every day in your job to form the basis of your Outline Format Federal resume.

Examples of hats:

- Supply Analyst
- Logistics Manager
- Transportation Specialist
- Supervisor
- Instructor
- Team Leader
- Database Administrator
- Researcher / Analyst
- Contract Officer
- Purchasing Specialist
- Office Administrator
- Advisor
- Computer Operations
- Customer Services
- Communications

Your list of hats:

____

____

____

____

____

____

____

CEDRICK SMITH
FEDERAL RESUME CASE STUDY #1 (RESUME PREVIEW)

Hiring Authority: US Navy 30% or More Disabled Veteran

Current Position: Administrative Officer/Ship's Secretary

Target: Technical Operations Group Assistant, GS-0303-7, Drug Enforcement Administration, GS-7

Greg Hall, Admin Officer, DEA San Diego Field Division, was mentoring Cedrick for a Direct Hire position within DEA. Greg saw that Cedrick's USAJOBS Federal resume was in the BIG BLOCK format, was very hard to read, and did not show the specialized experience for the position. **Kathryn Troutman, Federal Career Coach®, advised Cedrick to organize his USS Zumwalt experience into critical skills and accomplishments to feature Operations Technician experience.**

RESULTS

Cedrick would have been hired by Greg. But Cedrick found another Federal position before Greg and his office had a chance to offer him the position. Once Cedrick's resume was a Federal-style format, Cedrick was in-demand based on his experience.

QUALIFICATIONS REQUIRED

To qualify for this position at the GS-7 level, you must meet one of the following:

SPECIALIZED EXPERIENCE, TRAINING, AND CERTIFICATION REQUIREMENTS: You must have at least one (1) full year of specialized experience (equivalent to at least the GS-5 level in the Federal service) that has equipped you with the particular knowledge, skills, and abilities to successfully perform the duties of a Technical Operations Group Assistant. Specialized experience is experience in:

- Organization Liaison for Budget
- Organization Liaison for Purchasing
- Organizational Liaison for Human Resources
- Investigative Technology Program
- Correspondence Management, Reports, Logs Management
- Administrative and Office Operations
- Assist employees where there is no clear precedent

BEFORE AND AFTER KEYWORDS

BEFORE RESUME KEYWORDS

- ADMINISTRATIVE OFFICER
- SHIP'S SECRETARY
- FOLLOW COMMAND PROGRAMS
- RESPONSIBLE FOR LEADERSHIP
- USED AUTOMATED SYSTEMS
- MAINTAINED SENSITIVE
- RECORDS MANAGEMENT

AFTER KEYWORDS - *TARGETED*

- ORGANIZATIONAL LIAISON
- SUPERVISION & MANAGEMENT
- HUMAN RESOURCES ADMINISTRATION
- TECHNICAL SUPPORT
- AUTOMATED SYSTEMS EXPERTISE
- RECORDS MANAGEMENT OFFICER
- REGULATORY COMPLIANCE

BEFORE AND AFTER ORGANIZATION

BEFORE RESUME ORGANIZATION

- CONTACT INFORMATION
- WORK HISTORY

AFTER RESUME ORGANIZATION

- OBJECTIVE
- SPECIALIZED SKILLS
- WORK HISTORY
- KEY ACCOMPLISHMENTS

BEFORE RESUME

Cedrick's before Federal resume is in the BIG BLOCK format, and it's HARD TO READ.

Don't write your DUTIES in a BIG BLOCK! Too Hard to Read!

HINT

Cedrick E Smith, Jr.

1000 Way Drive
Chula Vista, CA 91915 United States
Mobile: 222-222-2222
Email: cedricke7@gmail.com

Work Experience:

USS ZUMWALT (DDG 1000)
Unit 100831 Box 1
FPO, AP 96693 United States

12/2017 - 11/2020
Salary: 88,989.00 USD Per Year
Hours per week: 80
Administrative Officer/Ship's Secretary
Duties, Accomplishments and Related Skills:
Managed the following Command programs; Family Care Plan, Exceptional Family Member, Personnel Security, Fitness Reports & Evaluations, Awards, Authorizing Official for Defense Travel System, Legal & Discipline, Command Travel Budget, Morale Welfare & Recreation. Managed and processed 100% of command Instructions, Notices and general correspondence for Command Triad & Department Head review and approval. Responsible for leadership, management and oversight of 4 personnel on all administrative functions. Used automated personnel systems to perform administrative human resource support functions (i.e, processing personnel actions, reviewing personnel information for discrepancies, maintain databases, and preparing reports, briefings, and correspondence, officer/enlisted pay issues and entitlements, e-leave). Maintained sensitive, highly confidential, personal and proprietary information with discretion and confidentiality for 160 personnel. Facilitated command level support to manage manpower and personnel transfers and indoctrination. Advanced interpersonal skills including verbal and written communication, active listening, critical thinking, persuasiveness, advising and counseling skills. Utilized standard office equipment (i.e., scanners, copiers, fax machines, and office automation systems) to perform a substantial range of office automation support functions. Records Management Officer - Established document and records management policies and processes. Ensured all personal data within the command's records system was safeguarded in accordance with the DoD Privacy Act. Ensured that the command remained in compliance with all Federal, Department of Navy, and Naval Facilities Engineering Command principles, techniques, policies, procedures, laws, and regulations to assist with document and records management programs. Applied Freedom of Information Act (FOIA) and Privacy Act (PA) principles as they related to document and records management processes and procedures. Assistant Command Security Manager - Responsible for the proper processing of security risk management guidance pertaining to the protection of advanced technology. Provide guidance in implementing security policy at government facilities. Provided guidance for the implementation of security policies at government facilities. Review documentation required for classified information systems in accordance with the current security regulations.

Developed and oversaw Security compliance inspections and self-inspections and developed corrective action plans. Lead and assisted with the investigations of security incidents to include initial reporting and documenting findings in accordance with applicable policies. Experience working with procedures and techniques in the area of physical, industrial, information and personnel security. Responsible for the review and application of governing policies to ensure command compliance and communicate orally and in writing to appropriate command level personnel. Instrumental in the personnel security program, utilizing JPAS /DISS to initiate, update and closeout personnel security investigations and visit requests. **Supervisor**: CAPT George Kent (666-555-4444)
Okay to contact this Supervisor: Yes

Navy Munitions Command Atlantic Det Bahrain

PSC 851 BOX 890

FPO, AE 09834 United States

10/2016 - 11/2017

Salary: 88,989.00 USD Per Year

Hours per week: 40
Administrative Officer
Duties, Accomplishments and Related Skills:
Managed the following Command programs; Family Care Plan, Exceptional Family Member, Personnel Security, Fitness Reports & Evaluations, Awards, Authorizing Official for Defense Travel System, Legal & Discipline, Command Travel Budget, Morale Welfare & Recreation. Managed and processed 100% of command Instructions, Notices and general correspondence for Command Triad & Department Head review and approval. Responsible for leadership, management and oversight of 2 personnel on all administrative functions. Used automated personnel systems to perform administrative human resource support functions (i.e, processing personnel actions, reviewing personnel information for discrepancies, maintain databases, and preparing reports, briefings, and correspondence, officer/enlisted pay issues and entitlements, e-leave). Maintained sensitive, highly confidential, personal and proprietary information with discretion and confidentiality for 45 personnel. Facilitated command level support to manage manpower and personnel transfers and indoctrination. Advanced interpersonal skills including verbal and written communication, active listening, critical thinking, persuasiveness, advising and counseling skills. Utilized standard office equipment (i.e., scanners, copiers, fax machines, and office automation systems) to perform a substantial range of office automation support functions. Records Management Officer- Established document and records management policies and processes. Ensured all personal data within the command's records system was safeguarded in accordance with the DoD Privacy Act. Ensured that the command remained in compliance with all Federal, Department of Navy, and Naval Facilities Engineering Command principles, techniques, policies, procedures, laws, and regulations to assist with document and records management programs. Applied Freedom of Information Act (FOIA) and Privacy Act (PA) principles as they related to document and records management processes and procedures. Detachment Security Manager-Responsible for the proper processing of security risk management guidance pertaining to the protection of advanced technology.

AFTER RESUME

Cedrick's after Federal resume is in the Outline Format, with his Qualifications in ALL CAPs. It will be much easier for HR to see that he is qualified for the position. This resume also has an impressive Accomplishments section.

CEDRICK SMITH

1111 San Diego Drive, San Diego, CA 90999
(666) 666-6666 csmith11@yahoo.com
30% or More Disabled Veteran

OBJECTIVE: Administrative Officer

SPECIALIZED SKILLS:

Organization Liaison
Budget Activities
Purchasing / Procurement
Human Resources
Computer Skills
Automation

WORK HISTORY:

USS ZUMWALT (DDG 1000) **12/2017–11/2020**
Unit 100831 Box 1 FPO, AP 96693 United States Hours per week: 40
Salary: 88,989.00 USD Per Year

Administrative Officer/Ship's Secretary
First Class Petty Officer, E-6

INTRODUCTION:

- The USS ZUMWALT was commissioned in Baltimore, MD, in 2016. As the first sole administrative officer for the ship in 2017, I performed all administrative support for 160 sailors on the ship for one year.
- After one year, I successfully submitted the justification and request to expand our manpower and was able to add two more personnel to form an administrative team.

ORGANIZATION LIAISON: Collaborated with Military Enlisted & Officer personnel, Federal Civilians & Contractors, and transferring service members from the Navy / Air Force Pacific for the ship's administrative operations. The ship deployed many times to complete tests of the ship's capabilities.

ALL CAPS KEYWORDS!

SUPERVISION & MANAGEMENT: Supervised four personnel on all administrative functions. Managed and processed 100% of command instructions, notices, and general correspondence for Command Triad & Department Head review and approval. Directed administrative and security support for physical, industrial, information and personnel security. Managed medical care, retention and promotion, and security of the 160 personnel assigned to the command.

All of the duty and accomplishment sentences are in past tense.

HUMAN RESOURCES ADMINISTRATION: Maintained sensitive, highly confidential, personal, and proprietary information with discretion and confidentiality for 160 personnel. Facilitated command level support to manage manpower and personnel transfers and indoctrination. Ensured indoctrination of new personnel to the ship, covering areas of pay benefits, support programs, medical coverage information, and retirement benefits.

TECHNICAL SUPPORT: As the program coordinator, ensured that all unmarried sailors with children had an approved family care plan on file. Ensured that all personnel completed the proper documentation and recertification for family members that were designated as exceptional for medical reasons. Reviewed and submitted annual fitness reports and evaluations for all personnel onboard.

Write 5 to 8 **Work History** duty paragraphs with ALL CAP HEADINGS.

AUTOMATED SYSTEMS EXPERTISE: Used automated personnel systems to perform administrative human resource support functions (processing personnel actions, reviewing personnel information for discrepancies, maintaining databases, and preparing reports, briefings, and correspondence, officer/enlisted pay issues and entitlements, e-leave). Systems expertise includes Windows & Mac Operating Systems; Computer Peripheral (Equipment) Operator; Microsoft Word, Excel, PowerPoint, Outlook; Google Drive, Docs, Sheets, Slides; SharePoint; Adobe; Calendar Management.

RECORDS MANAGEMENT OFFICER: Established document and records management policies and processes. Ensured all personal data within the command's records system were safeguarded in accordance with the Department of Defense (DoD) Privacy Act. Reviewed documentation required for classified information systems in accordance with the current security regulations. Ran compliance checks quarterly and reported findings.

REGULATORY COMPLIANCE: Ensured that the command remained in compliance with all Federal, Department of Navy, and Naval Facilities Engineering Command principles, techniques, policies, procedures, laws, and regulations to assist with document and records management programs. Applied Freedom of Information Act (FOIA) and Privacy Act (PA) principles.

COMMAND TRAVEL BUDGET: Managed a $100K travel budget to ensure that the agency maintained the appropriate number of specially trained personnel onboard. Coordinated flight and lodging requests for personnel and ensured proper account reconciliation after the completion of travel.

KEY ACCOMPLISHMENTS:

- Instrumental in the retention of personnel to ensure proper manning levels were maintained for ZUMWALT and the US Navy.
- Oversaw all aspects of the personnel security program, utilizing JPAS/DISS to initiate, update and close out personnel security investigations and visit requests.
- As President of the Morale Welfare & Recreation Committee, marshalled a 12-person team through the organization of multiple crew-focused events and tournaments, sourcing of new gym equipment, and the 2019 Spring Picnic and Command Holiday party, uplifting crew morale and generating over $12K to support the welfare of the ZUMWALT and her crew.

KEY ACCOMPLISHMENTS are featured here!

WHY GO GOVERNMENT?

Federal Employee Compensation Package: It's More than Just Salary

You're making a great choice when you choose a career with the Federal Government. You will find our comprehensive compensation and benefits package to be competitive. As a Federal employee, you and your family have access to a range of benefits that are designed to make your career rewarding while at the same time enabling you to balance work and family needs.

Compensation

- **Salary** — The Federal Government offers competitive base pay, with most positions using the General Schedule (GS) pay system. Some highly-competitive jobs, such as entry-level IT specialists, provide higher special pay rates.
- **Federal Student Loan Repayment** — Agencies may help repay your Federally-insured student loans up to a maximum of $10,000 a year or a $60,000 lifetime maximum.
- **Incentives and Awards** — In addition to salary, your hiring agency may offer monetary recruitment, relocation, or retention incentives and performance awards.

Leave and Workplace Flexibilities

- **Alternative Work Schedules** — Maintain valuable contributions to your work group while meeting your personal needs by operating on a non-traditional work schedule.
- **Vacation, Personal and Sick Time** — Enjoy paid and non-paid time off through our generous leave programs. You may also qualify for a higher leave accrual rate because of your non-federal work experience or uniformed service.
- Telework (external link) — The Federal Government is a leader in the use of innovative workplace arrangements like telework.

Additional Benefits

- 11 Paid Holidays
- Child Care Subsidies
- Child Care Workplace Flexibilities
- Commuter Subsidies (external link)
- Continuing Education and Professional Development
- Dental and Vision Insurance
- Elder Care Workplace Flexibilities
- Employee Assistance and Referral
- Family and Medical Leave Act (FMLA): A new paid leave benefit "paid parental leave" was made effective October 1, 2020, for qualifying FMLA purposes. This new leave benefit provides up to 12-weeks of paid leave. This leave in addition to an employee's earned annual and sick leave.
- Flexible Spending Accounts
- Health Insurance
- Leave to Care for Family Members
- Life Insurance
- Long-Term Care Insurance
- Pay and Leave Flexibilities
- Reasonable Accommodations
- Retirement Benefits
- Volunteer Activities/Community Service

From: *https://www.opm.gov/policy-data-oversight/pay-leave/pay-administration/fact-sheets/federal-employee-compensation-package/*

STEP 1
LEARN ABOUT FEDERAL JOBS

To get started on your Federal job search, you need to know some basic information about Federal jobs and how they are filled. In this step, we will give you a high-level overview. First, we'll ask you some questions about your job search. If you don't know the answers, don't worry. You'll be able to find much of the information as you go through this step.

ACTIVITY: Your Federal Job Search Goals

1. Job Titles and Series

What is your current military job title?

How many years of specialized experience do you have?

Which Federal job titles or series seem correct for you?

2. Grade and Salary

What is your current military rank?

What is your current military salary?

What is your target Federal grade level?

What is your target salary?

3. Agencies

What are your target agencies?

What types of Federal jobs can you apply for and how will you apply for them?

DIRECT HIRE PROCESS (FASTER HIRE PROCESS)

The chart below is a general overview of the **Direct Hire** process as prescribed by OPM. Average hire time can be 2 weeks to 50 days! This can be FAST. See the full process here:
https://www.opm.gov/policy-data-oversight/hiring-information/direct-hire-authority

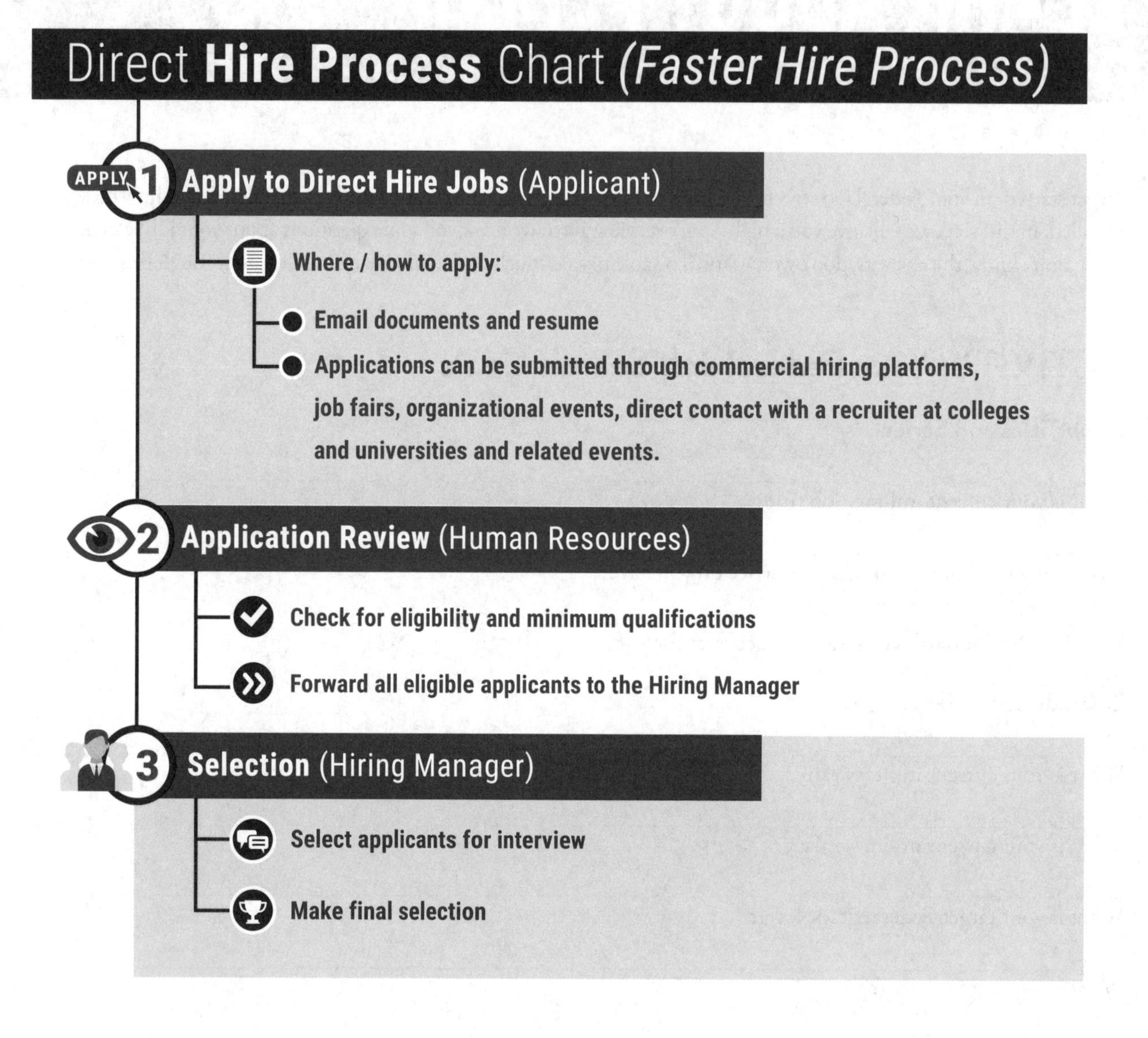

COMPETITIVE HIRING PROCESS

The chart below is a general overview of the competitive hiring process as prescribed by OPM. OPM states that this process takes 80 days from announcement closing to a Selection. See the full process here: *www.opm.gov/policy-data-oversight/human-capital-management/hiring-reform/hiring-process-analysis-tool/*

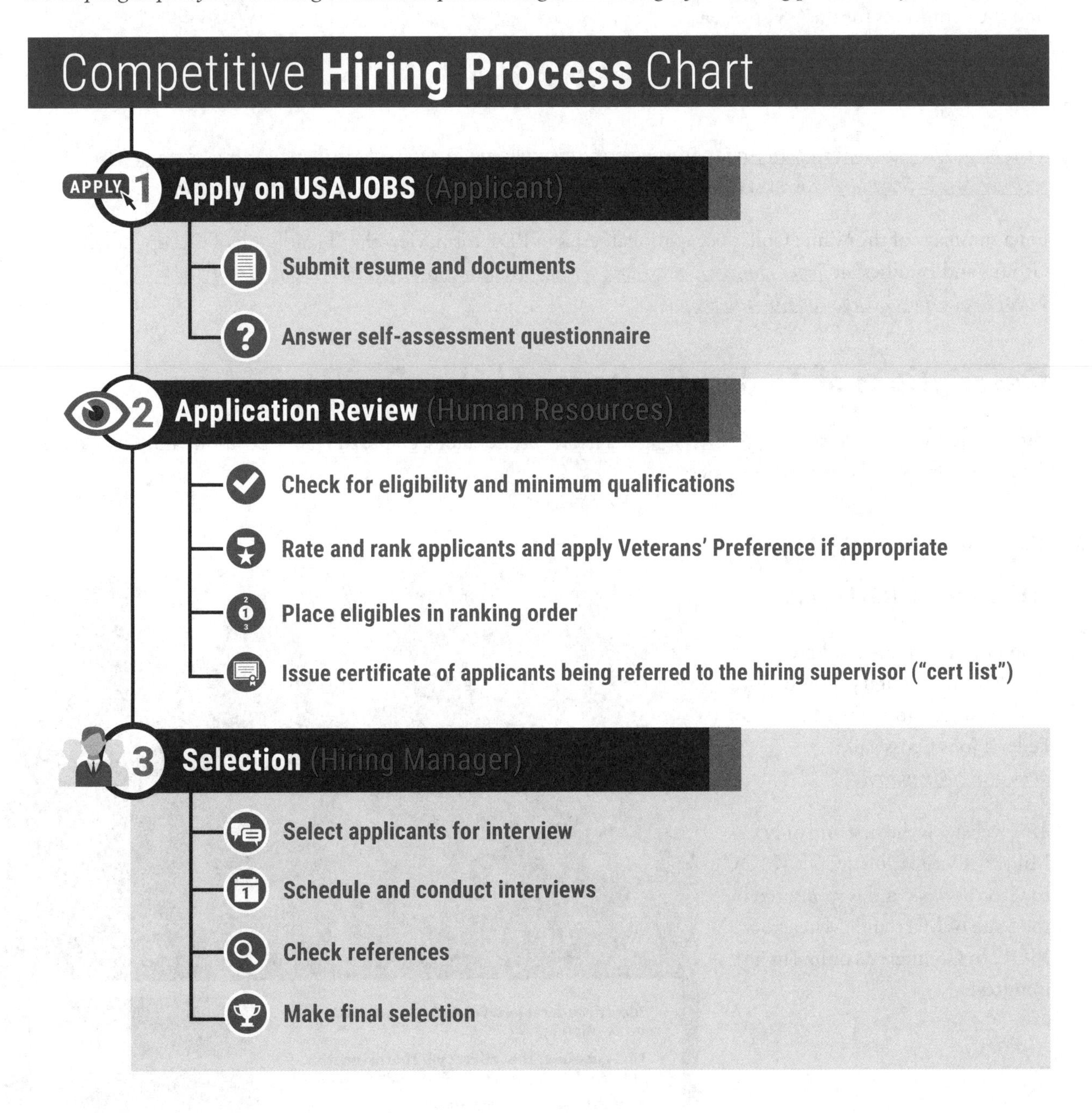

FEDERAL JOB TITLES AND SERIES

Most Federal jobs are defined as part of the General Schedule (GS) system and assigned a number and title. For example, GS-0341 is the Administrative Officer series. Visit the Office of Personnel Management (OPM) website to find the definitions for the GS positions.

NOTE: You can find Keywords for your resume in the OPM Standards.

Descriptions of White Collar Positions

Visit *https://www.opm.gov/policy-data-oversight/classification-qualifications/classifying-general-schedule-positions/#url=Standards* for a list of the GS white collar positions with links to the definitions and standards.

For a summary of the White Collar occupational series in PDF form, view the "Handbook of Occupational Groups and Families" at *www.opm.gov/policy-data-oversight/classification-qualifications/classifying-general-schedule-positions/occupationalhandbook.pdf*

Descriptions of Trades, Crafts, and Labor Positions

Visit *www.opm.gov/fedclass/html/fwseries.asp* for a listing of the trades, crafts, and labor positions and links to the definitions and standards for these series.

Translating Military into GS Positions

If you need to figure out how to translate your military position into a GS position, go to the Military to Federal Jobs Crosswalk: *www.mil2fedjobs.com*

This website is the first and only Military Occupational Code (MOC) to GS crosswalk and is sponsored by the State of Maryland. Match your MOC to GS interests online in just minutes!

GRADE AND SALARY

The General Schedule (GS) is a worldwide pay system that covers more than two million employees. The GS pay schedule has 15 grades and 10 steps in each grade covering more than 400 occupations. Pay varies by geographic location: Look up your potential salary WITH your locality pay. See the latest GS Pay Tables at: *https://www.opm.gov/policy-data-oversight/pay-leave/salaries-wages/*

Pay banding allows an organization to combine two or more grades into a wider "band" and is an increasingly popular alternative to the traditional GS system. The "grade" information may be specific to a particular agency.

Which grade you qualify for is based on the following:

Experience

- Quality of experience
- Directly related to the job or general nature of work
- Complexity of assignments (what, for whom, why)
- Decision-making authority or span of control
- Knowledge, skills, and abilities used
- Length of experience
- Full-time or part-time
- Number of hours per week

Education

- Major field of study
- Number of years or semester hours completed
- GPA

Training

- Related to job
- Number of days or hours

Qualifying Based on Education Alone

GS-2: High school graduation or equivalent (i.e., GED)

GS-3: 1 year above high school

GS-4: 2 years above high school (or Associate's degree)

GS-5: Bachelor's degree

GS 7: 1 full year of graduate study or Bachelor's degree with superior academic achievement (GPA 2.95 or higher out of a possible 4.0)

GS-9: Master's degree or equivalent such as J.D. or LL.B.

GS-11: Ph.D.

NOTE: There are exceptions to this chart; there are occupations that will not accept education in lieu of experience.

MILITARY RANK TO FEDERAL CIVILIAN GRADES

Determining the government grade level based on your military rank is challenging. Here are some ways to determine the appropriate grade.

Salary: Match the salary you are earning now against the OPM General Schedule charts.

Specialized Experience: Read USAJOBS announcements for the Specialized Experience required and see if you qualify for the grade level they are advertising.

Certification and Training: Read job announcements and see if you have the specific certification and training required.

Federal Civilian Grade	Wage Grade	Military Commissioned Officer	Military Warrant Officer	Military Enlisted
Assistants				Trainee/Assistants
GS-2, 3, 4, 5	WG-2, 3, 4, 5			E-2, 3, 4
GS-6, 7, 8	WG-6, 7, 8			E-5, 6
Specialist/ Technician		Junior Leaders / First-Line Supervisors		Specialist/First-Line Supervisors
GS-7	WG-9			E-3, 4
GS-9	WG-10	O-1		E-5, E-7
GS-11	WG-10	2	WO-1	E-5, E-7
GS-12	WG-10, 11, 12	3	WO-1	E-7
Team Lead/ Section Leader		Mid-Level Leader/ Section Manager		Operations Supervisor/ Supervisor of First-Line Supervisors
GS-12	WG-12	O-3, 4	WO-2	E-7, 8
GS-13	WG-12	4	3	E-8
Supervisor/ Branch Chief		Leader of Mid-Level Leaders /Manage Organizations		Superintendent/ Supervisor of Ops Supervisors
GS-13	WG-12, 13, 14	O-4	WO-4	E-8, 9
GS-14	WG-12, 13, 14	5	5	E-9
Manager		Senior Leader / Head of Organization		Senior Enl Advisor/ Career Field Manager
GS-14	WG-12, 13, 14	O-5	WO-5	
GS-15	WG-12, 13, 14	6		

NOTE: This chart is not an official Federal government grade to military rank conversion chart but an approximation based on our analysis of rank against the requirements of USAJOBS vacancy announcements. Conversions may vary.

FEDERAL AGENCIES

To find a complete list of Federal agencies, visit *www.usa.gov/federal-agencies*

Department of Defense (DOD)

DOD employs over three million military and civilians in three military departments (Army, Navy, and Air Force), the National Guard and various Reserves services, and a number of subordinate agencies.

For a listing of all DOD agencies, along with their job search URLs and a listing of the major types of positions that they employ, go to *www.resume-place.com/jsguide9*

Intelligence Community (IC)

In 2004, the Office of the Director of National Intelligence (ODNI) was established to manage IC efforts. The work of 17 civilian and military services IC agencies, branches, offices, and bureaus is now consolidated under the ODNI. Each of the organizations within the IC operates under its own directive.

For a listing of the IC organizations and a description of their mission, go to *www.resume-place.com/jsguide9*

Visit *www.intelligence.gov* for information on career opportunities in the 17 IC agencies across the U.S. and overseas. It is an excellent resource for exploring career choices and applying for positions. Some intelligence agencies offer internships and scholarship opportunities.

Excepted Service

Excepted service agencies (such as the Central Intelligence Agency and the Postal Service) do not post their positions on USAJOBS. To view a list of excepted service agencies and positions, go to *www.resume-place.com/jsguide9*

Non-Appropriated Funds (NAF) Jobs

NAF jobs are Federal jobs located on military bases worldwide. They are different from Federal civil service employment, because the monies used to pay the salaries of NAF employees come from a different source. NAF employees are paid from non-appropriated funds of Army & Air Force Exchange Service, Navy Exchange Service Command, Marine Corps exchanges, or any other armed forces organization for the comfort, pleasure, contentment, or physical or mental improvement of members of the military. Benefits are great! For a list of sites posting NAF jobs, visit *www.resume-place.com/jsguide9*

TYPES OF FEDERAL JOBS

Type of Federal Job	Some Features	Where to Find	Hiring Process	Does Veterans' Pref Apply?	Notes
Competitive Service Jobs	Must follow OPM hiring and personnel rules	USAJOBS or agency websites	Usually competitive: also, Direct Hire and special hiring paths available	YES for external announcements (open to all U.S. Citizens) NO for internal or merit announcements (open to Status Applicants)	Includes: VEOA, Direct Hire
Excepted Service Jobs	For unique qualification requirements or procedures (i.e., requires a polygraph) Hiring rules may differ	USAJOBS or agency websites	Depends on the agency; various tests; special criteria	Must view job announcement to determine how veterans will be considered	Includes: Pathways, VRA, 30% or more disabled vets, disabled vets enrolled in a training program, Special Appointing Authority for Certain Military Spouses, Schedule A and B, NAF, "Dual Status" Military Technicians
Senior Executive Service	For executive management positions	USAJOBS or agency websites	Competitive application reviewed by Agency Review Board and then Executive Review Board	No	More information in *The New SES Application 2nd Edition* by Kathryn Troutman and Diane Hudson

Special Hiring Paths

Due to numerous regulations, authorities, and exceptions based on unique situations, there may be different hiring scenarios not covered in the table above.

See page 28 for Special Hiring Paths list. Learn more by visiting the USAJOBS website at: *www.usajobs.gov/Help/working-in-government/unique-hiring-paths/*

VETERANS' PREFERENCE

How Is Veterans' Preference Applied to Public Job Announcements?

Non-disabled Veterans—If the resume is Qualified, the resume will rise to the top of the appropriate category based on your score!

Disabled Veterans—If the resume is scored and rated Qualified **(at least a score of 80)**, the resume will rise to the top of the highest category, Best Qualified!

Applications are reviewed, scored, and placed in one of three categories with a **CATEGORY RATING**: Qualified, Well-Qualified, or Best-Qualified.

Veterans' Preference gives eligible veterans preference in appointment over many other applicants. Veterans' Preference does not guarantee veterans a job, and it does not apply to internal agency actions such as promotions, transfers, reassignments, and reinstatements.

General Requirements

- Must have an honorable or general discharge.
- Retirees at O-5 or higher are not eligible for preference unless they are disabled veterans.
- Eligible veterans should claim preference on their application or resume.
- Applicants claiming 10-point preference must complete form SF-15.
- You must achieve a score of 80 or higher on your resume and application.

Types of Preference Eligibility

- Sole survivorship (0 point preference eligible)
- Non-disabled (5 point preference eligible)
- Disabled (10 point preference eligible)

For more information:

- *www.usajobs.gov/Help/working-in-government/unique-hiring-paths/veterans/*
- *www.fedshirevets.gov/*
- *www.military.com/benefits/veteran-benefits/veterans-employment-preference-points.html*

FAMILY MEMBER PREFERENCE (DERIVED PREFERENCE)

APPLICATION FOR 10-POINT VETERAN PREFERENCE
(TO BE USED BY VETERANS & RELATIVES OF VETERANS)

U.S. Office of Personnel Management — Form Approved: O.M.B. No. 3206-0001

PERSON APPLYING FOR PREFERENCE

1. Name *(Last, First, Middle)*

2. Home address *(Street Number, City, State and ZIP Code)*

VETERAN INFORMATION ***(to be provided by person applying for preference)***

3. Veteran's name *(Last, First, Middle)* exactly as it appears on Service Records

4. Periods of service

Branch of service	Date entered active duty	Date Separated or Released from Active Duty (if applicable)

Download the application: *https://www.opm.gov/forms/pdf_fill/SF15.pdf*

- SPOUSES
- WIDOWS/WIDOWERS
- PARENTS OF DECEASED VETS
- PARENTS OF DISABLED VETS
- MILITARY SPOUSES

Derived Preference

On October 7, 2015, the President signed the "Gold Star Fathers Act of 2015," and into law. The Act became effective on January 7, 2016 and amends section 2108(3)(F) and (G) of Title 5, United States Code, by expanding preference eligibility from the "mother" of a deceased or disabled veteran who is unable to use his or her preference, to the "parent" of that service member. OPM is in the process of updating the SF-15, Application for 10-point Veterans' Preference; and relevant website pages. The requirements are described in an OPM memorandum to Chief Human Capital Officers concerning this new authority.

Derived Preference is a method where you, as the spouse, widow/widower, or parent of a veteran may be eligible to claim veterans' preference when the veteran is unable to use it. You will be given XP Preference (10 points) in appointment if you meet the eligibility criteria.

Both a parent and a spouse (including widow or widower) may be entitled to preference on the basis of the same veteran's service if each meets the requirements applicable to a parent and a spouse, respectively.

NOTE: The derived preference for spouses is different than the preference the Department of Defense is required by law to extend to spouses of active duty members in filling its civilian positions. For more information on that program, contact your local Department of Defense personnel office.

Spouses

As a spouse of a veteran, you will be eligible for derived preference if the veteran has been unable to qualify for a Federal position along the general lines of his or her usual occupation because of a service-connected disability. Such a disqualification may be presumed when the veteran is unemployed and

- is rated by appropriate military or Department of Veterans Affairs authorities to be 100% disabled and/or unemployable; OR
- has retired, been separated, or resigned from a civil service position on the basis of a disability that is service-connected in origin; OR
- has attempted to obtain a civil service position or other position along the lines of his or her usual occupation and has failed to qualify because of a service-connected disability.

Widows/Widowers

As a widow or widower of a veteran, you will be eligible if you and the veteran did not divorce, you have not remarried, or any remarriage was annulled, and the veteran

- served during a war or during the period April 28, 1952 through July 1, 1955, or in a campaign or expedition for which a campaign medal has been authorized; OR
- died while on active duty that included service described immediately above under conditions that would not have been the basis for other than an honorable or general discharge.

Parent of a Deceased Veteran

As the parent of a veteran, you will be eligible if your son or daughter lost his or her life under honorable conditions while serving in the armed forces during a war, or during the period April 28, 1952 through July 1, 1955, or in a campaign or expedition for which a campaign medal has been authorized; AND

- Your own spouse is totally and permanently disabled; OR
- At the time, when preference is claimed, you are unmarried or, if married, legally separated from your spouse.

Parent of a Disabled Veteran

Alternatively, you will be eligible if your son or daughter was separated with an honorable or general discharge from active duty, including training service in the Reserves or National Guard, and is permanently and totally disabled from a service-connected injury or illness; AND

- Your own spouse is totally and permanently disabled; OR
- At the time when preference is claimed, you are unmarried or, if married, legally separated from your spouse.

WHEN TO APPLY FOR TRANSITIONING AND RETIRING MILITARY

You can apply for Federal jobs BEFORE you retire or separate!

Apply for Federal Positions within 120 days of Separation or Retirement

- The military separatee or retiree will need a **Proof of Service or Statement of Service Letter** from their Executive Officer or military personnel office.
- Military separatees and retirees (except for military retirees applying for DOD positions: see 180-Day Waiver below) can apply for Federal positions within 120 days of separation or retirement.
- A military retiree who is 120 days from retirement CAN apply to non-DOD agencies, such as the FBI, DOC, or DOT, using the Proof or Statement of Service.
- Make sure to upload your Proof or Statement of Service, with a copy of your separation or retirement order, into your USAJOBS documents.
- When you receive your DD-214, upload it, then delete your Proof or Statement of Service and separation or retirement order.

180-Day Waiver Needed for Retirees to Begin a DOD Job

- Retiring military personnel cannot begin federal employment with a Department of Defense agency until 180 days past their retirement date.
- Exceptions to this policy will require the DOD agency to submit a waiver to the 180-day policy proving that there were no non-vet applicants qualified to fill the position under normal merit rules.
- Members should not assume that they can submit/request the 180-day waiver; submission is up to the agency.
- Read the guidance on the 180-day waiver policy here: *www.resume-place.com/jsguide9*

STEP 2

NETWORK & USE NON-COMPETITIVE HIRING

Networking works for government job search. In this step you will learn about the Special Hiring Authorities where managers can hire directly. You will learn about the Direct Hire Authority which is a special hiring program for hiring with USAJOBS and outside of the online application system. Knowing managers can be an advantage for getting hired into government. It's a good idea to network and to apply for jobs on USAJOBS!

Can you get hired outside of USAJOBS? YES!

MYTH: You can only get a Federal job through the standard application method.
FACT: There are other ways to get a Federal job.

Most people miss this VERY important point: **YOU CAN GET HIRED OUTSIDE OF USAJOBS APPLICATIONS.** We call these other routes networking and non-competitive hiring. Networking can include going to a job fair, where they may give tentative job offers, or emailing an HR specialist or Selective Placement Program Manager. A trend we are seeing is that Direct Hire Authority is a non-competitive hiring tool that is much more commonly used than before as a way to hire individuals from outside of the traditional USAJOBS application method.

By networking and reaching out to contacts in the Federal government, you can

- Find out about government hiring
- Discover job opportunities that you do not see on USAJOBS.gov
- Get hired WITHOUT going through the formal competitive hiring process.

> **THE CAVEAT:** Remember, your federal resume MUST show the qualifications for the position to get Best Qualified and hired non-competitively!

Ways to Get Hired **Non-Competitively**

1. Find a POSITION that can be filled non-competitively.

Everyone	DIRECT HIRE

& Use a SPECIAL HIRING AUTHORITY to be hired non-competitively for competitive positions.

Group	Special Hiring Authority
Veterans	30+% Disabled Veterans' Preference; Veterans Readjustment Act (VRA)
Family Members	Family Member Preference (Derived Preference)
Military Spouses	Military spouses of active duty military (EO 13473, Military Spouse Program)
People with Disabilities	Schedule A Hiring Authority for People with Disabilities
Students & Recent Graduates	Post-Secondary Direct Hire Authority (Pathways)
Returning overseas employees & family members	Family Members of Overseas Government Employees & Foreign Service Return Workers

NON-COMPETITIVE HIRING PROGRAMS

Direct Hire

- Direct Hire Authority (DHA) is a special hiring authority created to help agencies fill vacancies in the competitive service under certain circumstances, such as filling critical skills gaps or a severe shortage of candidates.
- DHA can be determined by the Office of Personnel Management (OPM) when there is either a severe shortage of candidates or a critical hiring need for such positions or Congress can also provide DHA directly to departments and/or agencies for specified purposes.
- DHA expedites hiring by eliminating competitive ranking and rating procedures and veterans' preference.

How to Network for Direct Hire Positions

Networking Strategy	What to Do
Job Expo	Attend a job expo and take your two- to three-page networking resume. Also bring your supporting documentation for the agency representative or recruiter.
LinkedIn	Update your LinkedIn account. Research specific agency managers or human resources specialists and contact them through LinkedIn to see if you can write to them directly regarding a Federal position.
Cover Letter	Send a customized cover letter that will specify the types of positions, salary, grade levels, and locations you are seeking.
Follow-up	This is critical! If you do not hear from them, be sure to follow up.

NOTE: See the DIRECT HIRE hiring process on page 14!

SPECIAL HIRING PATHS

On USAJOBS, special hiring paths are ways that you can use special hiring authorities to be hired non-competitively. Do you qualify for any of these paths? If so, then you have an opportunity to network for your Federal job!

The Public
U.S. citizens, nationals, or those who owe allegiance to the U.S.

Veterans
Veterans of the U.S. Armed Forces.

National Guard & Reserves
Current members, those who want to join or transitioning military members.

Senior executives
Individuals looking for an executive level job.

Family of overseas employees
Family members of a federal employee or uniformed service member who is, or was, working overseas.

Peace Corps & AmeriCorps VISTA
Individuals who have served at least 2 years with the Peace Corps or 1 year with AmeriCorps VISTA.

Federal employees
Current or former federal employees in the competitive or excepted services.

Military spouses
Military spouses relocating under PCS orders, or whose spouse is 100% disabled or died while on active duty.

Students & recent graduates
Current students enrolled in or who have graduated from an accredited educational institution

Individuals with disabilities
Individuals who are eligible under Schedule A.

Native Americans
Native Americans or Alaskan Natives with a tribal affiliation.

Special authorities
Individuals eligible under a special authority not listed above, but defined in the federal hiring regulations.

Read more at: *www.usajobs.gov/Help/working-in-government/unique-hiring-paths/*

Veterans' Readjustment Act (VRA)

Under the VRA, eligible veterans can be appointed without competition to a white-collar position through GS 11. You are eligible if you

- Received a campaign badge for service during a war or in a campaign or expedition
- Are a disabled veteran
- Received an Armed forces Service Medal for participation in a military operation
- Are a recently separated veteran (within the last 3 years), AND separated under honorable conditions (this means an honorable or general discharge)

30% or More Disabled Veterans' Preference

The 30% or More Disabled Veteran authority allows an agency to appoint without competition any veteran with a 30% or more service-connected disability. You are eligible if you

- Retired from active military service with a service-connected disability rating of 30% or more
- Have a rating by the Department of Veterans Affairs showing a compensable service-connected disability of 30% or more

There is no grade level restriction. This authority can be used to make temporary (at least 60 days but not to exceed 1 year) or term (more than 1 year, but not more than 4) appointments in the competitive service. An agency has the authority to convert such a position to a permanent position if it chooses to do so. When the authority is used to meet a time-limited need, however, you will not be converted to a permanent appointment.

Veterans Employment Opportunities Act (VEOA)

VEOA is different from the other hiring authorities listed in this section in that it does not allow you to be hired non-competitively, but it is an important opportunity to be aware of.

VEOA provides preference eligibles and certain eligible veterans the opportunity to compete for certain positions announced under an agency's merit promotion procedures. It applies only when the agency is filling a permanent, competitive service position and has decided to solicit candidates from outside its own workforce. It allows eligible veterans and preference eligibles to apply to announcements that would otherwise be open to so called "status" candidates, i.e., "current competitive service employees and certain prior employees who have earned competitive status."

To be eligible to be considered pursuant to VEOA appointment, your latest discharge must be issued under honorable conditions (this means an honorable or general discharge), AND you must be either preference eligible or a veteran who substantially completed 3 or more years of active service under honorable conditions.

When agencies recruit from outside their own workforce under merit promotion procedures, their announcements must state VEOA is applicable. As a VEOA eligible, you are not subject to geographic area of consideration limitations. When applying under VEOA, you must rate and rank among the best qualified applicants, overall, to be considered for appointment.

Military Spouses of Active Duty Military (EO 13473)

Under this authority, a hiring manager may appoint without competition a military spouse who meets certain criteria to any position in the competitive service for which they are qualified. The authority does not entitle spouses to an appointment over any other applicant—it is used at the discretion of an agency. There is no limit on grade level. You are eligible if you are a:

- Spouse of a member of the armed forces on active duty

Family Members of Overseas Government Employees and Foreign Service Return Workers

You may be eligible to be hired without competition if you worked overseas as an appropriated fund Federal employee while a family member of a civilian, non-appropriated fund, or uniformed service member serving overseas, for an accumulated total of 52 weeks and received a fully successful (pass) or better performance appraisal. This appointment eligibility is effective for a period of 3 years following the date of return from overseas to the United States.

You must provide a copy of a recent SF-50 Notification of Personnel Action to support your claim, and a copy of your most recent performance appraisal.

Schedule A Hiring Authority for People with Disabilities

Schedule A is a special appointing authority allowing agencies to appoint without competition individuals, including eligible veterans, who have a severe physical, psychiatric, or intellectual disability. You must provide a copy of the letter documenting your disability from a licensed professional.

Post-Secondary Direct Hire Authority for Students and Recent Graduates (Pathways)

Agencies may hire qualified graduates to a position in the competitive service classified in a professional or administrative occupational category at the GS–11 level, or an equivalent level, or below.

Minimum qualifications:

1. Have received a baccalaureate or graduate degree from an institution of higher education
2. Apply for the position within 2 years of receiving degree OR within 4 of 12 years of obligated service in a uniformed service (and not later than 2 years after the date of the discharge or release of the individual from that service)
3. Meet each minimum qualification standard in the vacancy announcement

NETWORKING FOR SPECIAL HIRING PATHS

Here are some ideas to get you started with networking:

Networking Strategy	What to Do
Resume	Clearly indicate at the top of your resume which hiring authority you qualify for.
Email	Send your introductory cover letter, Federal resume, and appropriate documentation to the Veterans' Representatives, Selective Placement Program Coordinator, or HR Specialist to introduce your skills and interest in a position at their agency.
Job Expo	Take your two- to three-page networking resume. Also take your supporting documentation for the agency representative or recruiter.
LinkedIn	Update your LinkedIn account. Research specific agency managers or human resources specialists and contact them through LinkedIn to see if you can write to them directly regarding a Federal position using one of the non-competitive hiring authorities.
Cover Letter	Send a customized cover letter that will specify the types of positions, salary, grade levels, and locations you are seeking.
Follow-up	This is critical! If you do not hear from them, be sure to follow up.

Add your hiring authority / preference after your personal information

JEREMIAH JONES
1010 Nottingham Street
Boston, MA 20202
(443) 444-4444
Jjones123@gmail.com

Eligible for Veterans' Preference and VRA
Eligible for 30% or More Disabled Veterans Preference and VRA
Eligible for EO 13473, US Army Military Active Duty Spouse
Eligible or Derived Preference (of 100% Disabled, unable to work in previous career spouse or child)
Eligible for Schedule A Hiring
Eligible for Post-Secondary Direct Hire Authority for Students and Recent Graduates
Eligible for Foreign Service Family Member
Eligible for Returning Peace Corps Volunteers

STEP 2

NETWORKING CONTACTS

Selective Placement Program Coordinators

If you are a 30% or more disabled veteran, or a person with a targeted disability, you could network with Selective Placement Program Coordinators to inquire about opportunities for being hired non-competitively.

A directory of coordinators is available at *www.opm.gov/policy-data-oversight/disability-employment/selective-placement-program-coordinator/*

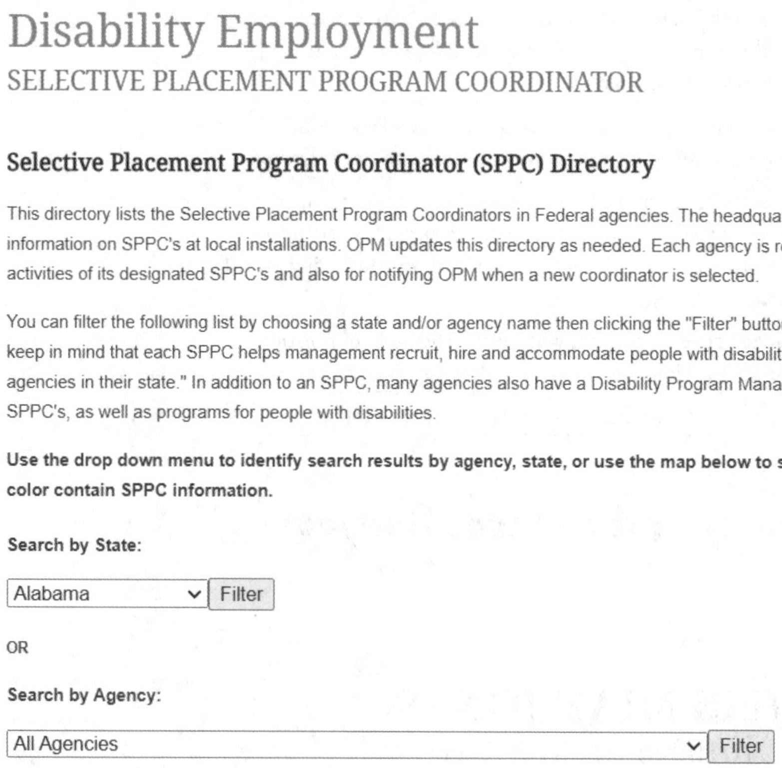

Disability Employment

SELECTIVE PLACEMENT PROGRAM COORDINATOR

Selective Placement Program Coordinator (SPPC) Directory

This directory lists the Selective Placement Program Coordinators in Federal agencies. The headquarters SPPC's can provide information on SPPC's at local installations. OPM updates this directory as needed. Each agency is responsible for monitoring the activities of its designated SPPC's and also for notifying OPM when a new coordinator is selected.

You can filter the following list by choosing a state and/or agency name then clicking the "Filter" button. When searching by state, please keep in mind that each SPPC helps management recruit, hire and accommodate people with disabilities for their agency only, not for all agencies in their state." In addition to an SPPC, many agencies also have a Disability Program Manager who manage and evaluate SPPC's, as well as programs for people with disabilities.

Use the drop down menu to identify search results by agency, state, or use the map below to select a state. States with a green color contain SPPC information.

Search by State:

Alabama Filter

OR

Search by Agency:

All Agencies Filter

Veterans' Representatives

If you are a veteran, you can network with agency Veterans' Representatives directly to find out if there are opportunities for being hired non-competitively: *https://www.fedshirevets.gov/veterans-council/agency-directory/*

Write to these Veterans' Representatives directly. Include your resume, cover letter, and DD-214, Statement of Service and/or VA letter.

Hiring Managers and Human Resources Specialists

If you are a candidate for any of the Special Hiring Authorities, you can contact a Hiring Manager or an HR Specialist DIRECTLY (or talk to them at a job fair) about non-competitive Federal positions that may not be advertised on USAJOBS. They could use your special hiring program to consider you for a Federal position.

MAXINE GOMEZ
FEDERAL RESUME CASE STUDY #2

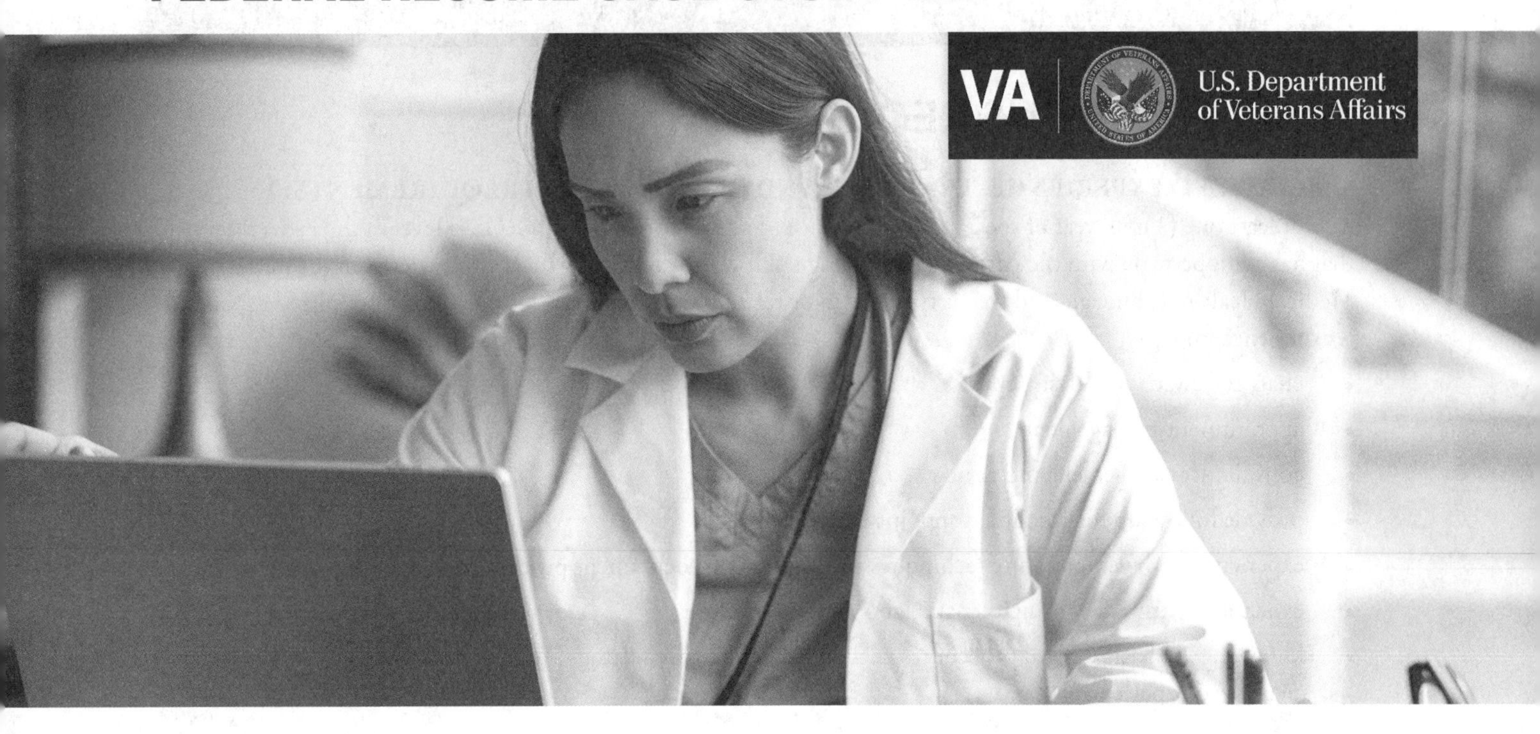

Hiring Authority: US Army Derived Preference. Husband is 100% Disabled and Unable to Work.

Last Position: Direct Support Manager (Licensed Certified Nursing Assistant)

Target: Seeking First Federal Position—Health Technician, GS-5, Veterans Administration, Palo Alto, CA.

Kathryn Troutman, Federal Career Coach® and Caregiver, coached Maxine to expand her descriptions in the resume to include real healthcare and clinical scenarios, relevant skills, and basically MATCH the job announcement. "I would like to leverage my nursing assistant experience to get an entry level job at the Palo Alto VA hospital. Due to my husband being deemed unemployable by the VA, I would like to exercise his 10 point veterans' preference." Maxine needed the Federal position because of the retirement, leave, and flexibility of a Federal position, while being a caregiver for her US Army Retired husband.

RESULTS **SELECTED**

Maxine was hired and able to grow within the VA system. In this position, she has the flexibility she needs for caregiving, plus promotion potential for her career.

Health Technician

DEPARTMENT OF VETERANS AFFAIRS

Veterans Health Administration

QUALIFICATIONS REQUIRED

SPECIALIZED EXPERIENCE, TRAINING, AND CERTIFICATION REQUIREMENTS: You must have at least one (1) full year of specialized experience (equivalent to at least the GS-4 level in the Federal service) that has equipped you with the particular knowledge, skills, and abilities to successfully perform the duties of a Medical Health Technician, and that is typically in or related to the work of this position. Specialized experience is experience in:

- chart review, data analysis reports
- appointment management
- consultant management and review
- provide follow-up for scheduled appointments
- experience with venipuncture techniques and specimen procurement procedures
- experience with safety principles and laboratory procedures
- knowledge of basic clerical procedures needed in a laboratory setting. (Your resume must document your specialized experience.)

BEFORE AND AFTER KEYWORDS

BEFORE RESUME KEYWORDS

- RELIABLE, SERVICE-FOCUSED REGISTERED NURSING PROFESSIONAL
- PATIENT CARE & SAFETY
- ASSISTED INDIVIDUALS TO ADJUST TO LIFE
- CONTRIBUTED TO INDIVIDUALS IN MONITORING AND/OR ADMINISTERING MEDICATIONS
- CONDUCTED FIRE DRILLS AND MANAGED EMERGENCY SITUATIONS
- REMOVED DEFECTIVE EQUIPMENT, REPORTED HAZARDS
- MONITORED AND DOCUMENTED PATIENT INTAKE AND OUTPUT

AFTER KEYWORDS - *TARGETED*

- CHART REVIEW AND DATA ANALYSIS REPORTS
- APPOINTMENT MANAGEMENT
- VENIPUNCTURE TECHNIQUES
- SPECIMEN PROCUREMENT PROCEDURES
- SAFETY PRINCIPLES
- CLERICAL PROCEDURES IN LABORATORY SETTING

BEFORE AND AFTER ORGANIZATION

BEFORE RESUME ORGANIZATION

- OBJECTIVE
- SKILLS
- WORK HISTORY
- EDUCATION
- REFERENCES

AFTER RESUME ORGANIZATION

- SUMMARY OF QUALIFICATIONS
- PROFESSIONAL EXPERIENCE
- EDUCATION / CERTIFICATIONS & LICENSES

FEDERAL RESUME COACHING WITH THE KSAs

C) Demonstrated Knowledge, Skills, and Abilities (KSAs). YOU HAVE TO WRITE ABOUT THESE IN THE RESUME – AND EVEN GIVE EXAMPLES.

- **KSA 1** - Ability to assist in the full range of nursing care to patients/residents with physical and/or behavioral problems in a hospital, long term care or outpatient setting under the direction of a Registered Nurse and/or Licensed Vocational Nurse/Licensed Practical Nurse.
  You have the CAN Certification right? Is this relevant here?

- **KSA 2** - Ability to communicate orally with patients/residents, families, interdisciplinary team and other personnel. This includes serving as a preceptor to new [NAs] by assisting with the coordination of their orientation and overseeing/assessing their practical experience while in a clinical setting.
  Have you helped with mentoring new hires in the nursing home or the group home?

- **KSA 3** - Ability to recognize and react to emergent patient/resident care situations and intervene while waiting for assistance. For example, recognizing need for basic life support, controlling bleeding and assisting with behavior crisis, etc.
  I am sure you have had the opportunity to react to emergent patient care situations and intervene while waiting for assistance. Can you give examples?

YOUR TURN .... THINK ABOUT THIS:

Can you give examples of your group home residents or your nursing home patients who had critical need situations, requiring decisive actions, and follow-up? *–Kathryn*

BEFORE RESUME

This resume is not targeted toward Health Technician, GS-5. This is a good two-page resume, but it does not include the keywords for the job announcement. The AFTER resume will include specific caregiving examples and expand the technical duties to match the announcement.

MAXINE GOMEZ
10100 Looseleaf Road
Cupertino, CA 95014
(777) 777-7777
MaxineG11@gmail.com

OBJECTIVE Reliable, service-focused registered nursing professional with excellent patient-care and charting skills gained through ten years of CNA and Direct Support experience. Compassionate and technically skilled in attending to patients in diverse healthcare settings including Dementia and Mental Disabilities. BLS and CPR certified (current).

SKILLS

Patient Care & Safety	Vital Signs & Patient Monitoring
Patient Advocacy and Support	Medication Administration
Medical Terminology	Privacy / HIPAA Regulations
Electronic Medical Records	

WORK HISTORY DIRECT SUPPORT MANAGER – HOFFMANCARE ASSOCIATES – MOUNT JOY, PA 12/2013 – 02/2017

Assisted individuals to adjust to life as an independent member of the community. Supported individuals where applicable in the management of the symptoms of their mental illness and establish their own recovery plan. Contributed to individuals in monitoring and/or administering medications. Brought up-to-date and completed all daily, weekly, and monthly records, reports, logs, progress notes, location reports, and medical records in a timely fashion.

Connected and collaborated with on-site team, individual's family, involved agencies, and the community in providing relevant information when needed and applicable. Managed and/or finalized all duties and responsibilities in the daily operation of the residence in the 24-hour daily operation of the residence. Conducted fire drills and managed emergency situations during shift. Adhered to all state, local and federal to Public Health and Welfare Regulatory laws and regulations. Encouraged and helped residents adhere to all dietary guidelines. Maintains the physical environment in a manner that does not create a health and safety risk for others. Transported residents to services/appointment in personal vehicle and assisted individuals in and out of vehicles. Performed other duties as assigned daily.

SUPERVISORY CERTIFIED NURSES ASSISTANT- HRC MANORCARE – LANCASTER, PA 02/2011 – 05/2012

Removed defective equipment, reported hazards, observed safety regulations, contributed to infection control, and utilized proper aseptic technique in performance of duties. Entered information about the residents' condition in the chart, utilizing appropriate formats.

CERTIFIED NURSES ASSISTANT- CENTRAL PENN NURSING CARE – LANCASTER, PA 01/2010 – 02/2011

Monitored and documented patient intake and output. Worked on small group activities with residents according to the patients/resident treatment plan. Utilized glucose monitoring machine to receive glucose readings for residents. Provided direct care for complex residents. Verbally provided patient information to the treatment team for inclusion in the residents' plan of care, participated in treatment team meetings for resident care planning. Actively participated in Treatment Planning Meetings. Participated in maintaining a clean, safe environment for the patient/resident. Communicated effectively with patients/residents, their families and other health professionals.

EDUCATION

ASSOCIATES OF SCIENCE IN MEDICAL ASSISTING TECHNOLOGY – KEISER UNIVERSITY – IN PROGRESS

CERTIFIED NURSES ASSISTANT – HARRISBURG AREA COMMUNITY COLLEGE – 2006

Expert knowledge on providing care and assisting clients who cannot care for themselves, measuring and recording vital signs, assisting clients with bathing, dressing, feeding and toileting. Other relevant coursework including: caring for clients with catheters, providing range of motion exercises, transporting clients in wheelchairs, make beds, providing infection control and safety awareness and providing post-mortem care. Pennsylvania Registered Nurse Aide - License Number: 999999; Original Issue Date - 03-19-2007; Expiration Date - 03-18-2023

GENERAL EDUCATION DIPLOMA – PA DEPARTMENT OF EDUCATION – 06/2005

REFERENCES Will Furnish Upon Request

AFTER RESUME

This AFTER resume is now targeted toward the qualifications required for the position. The sections are reorganized to feature relevant education, skills, and experience.

MAXINE GOMEZ, CNA

10100 Looseleaf Road, Unit G | Cupertino, CA 95014
Cell Phone: 777-777-7777 | maxg@yahoo.com

Derived Veterans' Preference, VEOA: 10 Points

SUMMARY OF QUALIFICATIONS

Dedicated, compassionate Certified Nursing Assistant (CNA) with over 10 years of professional experience providing physical care and assistance to patients with all Activities of Daily Living (ADL). Skilled in providing the full range of nursing care to patients/residents with physical and behavioral problems in long term care settings, including nursing homes and residential care facilities. Understanding of regulatory compliance, including HIPAA. Proficient in EMR/EHR systems. High ethical standards. Registered Nursing Professional. BLS and CPR certified.

PROFESSIONAL EXPERIENCE

DIRECT SUPPORT MANAGER (Licensed Certified Nursing Assistant) 12/2018 – 01/2021
Houghlan Care Associates Hours per Week: 40
100 S Tramble St, Reading, PA 17552
Supervisor name: Ellen Masters (777) 222-2222; Permission to Contact

MANAGED THE DELIVERY OF HIGH QUALITY, COMPASSIONATE PHYSICAL CARE AND ASSISTANCE to 20 residents at Hoffman Care Associates, a licensed residential care facility that provides community and residential-based services to physically and intellectually disabled patients. Assisted patients with adjusting to life as an independent member of the community.

CHART REVIEW AND DATA ANALYSIS REPORTS: Provided support for the daily management of mental disorder symptoms and behavioral problems and assisted in establishing recovery plans. Supervised 10 caregivers companywide. Provided technical guidance and training.

SKILLFULLY PROVIDED PHYSICAL CARE AND ASSISTANCE TO RESIDENTS: Assisted with bathing, showering, shaving, grooming, feeding, ambulating, weighing, and maintaining appropriate skin care precautions. Ensured adherence to established dietary guidelines. Assisted with monitoring and administering prescribed medications. Drew on 10+ years of CNA experience to identify basic normal versus abnormal vital signs to adapt patient care activities.

CHART REVIEW AND DATA ANALYSIS REPORTS: Transported residents to services and appointments. Assisted with getting into and out of vehicles. Assisted in transferring and transporting medically compromised and seriously ill patients to tests and procedures using gurneys and wheelchairs.

SAFETY PRINCIPLES: Communicated daily with residents, families, interdisciplinary healthcare team, peers, and other support personnel. Served as a preceptor to new caregiving assistants. Assisted with orientation and assessed their experience in delivering care.

CLERICAL PROCEDURES IN LABORATORY SETTING: Assured the timely update and completion of all records, reports, logs, progress notes, location reports, and medical records. Collaborated with the on-site team, the resident's family, associated agencies, and the community in providing relevant information when needed and applicable. Applied knowledge of the Health Insurance Portability and Accountability Act (HIPAA) to protect the privacy of a patient's health information. Ensured adherence with local, state, and federal regulations and quality standards.

EMERGENT PATIENT CARE: Managed intervention of multiple emergent patient care situations, including the following:
-- PATIENT PROFILE: 64-year-old intellectually disabled male with type I diabetes, early onset Alzheimer's disease, and seizure disorder.

- While assisting the resident with Activities of Daily Living (ADL) one evening, he experienced a seizure. I observed his condition had become unstable and lowered him to the floor before his legs became unsteady. I called for assistance from another staff member and continued to measure the duration of the seizure. We followed his seizure medical protocol and called his physician. After the seizure ended, I asked appropriate questions and documented his answers. The resident was able to speak with his physician. Post-seizure, I used a glucose monitor to check the resident's blood sugar, morning and evening, as required by his new care plan.

-- PATIENT PROFILE: 32-year-old male resident with an intellectual disability, Muscular Dystrophy, and a tracheostomy tube; required a feeding tube and oxygen.

- I assisted with tube feeding, flushing the feeding tube, and cleaning, suctioning, and changing the inner cannula of the trach tube. This resident was only able to transfer and walk with assistance and was slowly losing his ability to walk. One evening, as a staff member was transferring the resident from his wheelchair to the bed, the feeding tube was pulled out. I was called by the distraught staff to provide assistance. I quickly calmed the resident and staff member. I called EMS, and the resident was transported for reinsertion of the feeding tube. I prepared an incident report and charted the events. Training was subsequently provided to all direct support staff on the proper protocol for the resident's feeding tube.

CERTIFIED NURSING ASSISTANT (CNA) 02/2015 – 05/2018
TBC HealthServices Hours per Week: 40
200 Smith Road, Lancaster, PA 17603
Supervisor: Melissa Rodriguez, 717-333-4444; Do not contact

CERTIFIED NURSING ASSISTANT and member of the nursing team at HRC Manor Care HealthServices, a skilled nursing care facility with 172 beds. Worked under the direction of a

Registered Nurse (RN), Licensed Vocational Nurse (LVN)/Licensed Practical Nurse (LPN) to provide the full range of nursing care to patients with a wide range of physical and behavioral problems.

AS AN INTEGRAL MEMBER OF THE NURSING TEAM, PROVIDED PHYSICAL CARE AND ASSISTANCE to patients, to include bathing, showering, shaving, grooming, feeding, ambulating, and weighing. Properly positioned patients with prescribed physical limitations. Instructed and guided patients in developing cleanliness and sound health practices in all aspects of daily living. Maintained appropriate skin care precautions. Assisted with admissions, transfers, discharges, and postmortem care. Managed a daily patient load of 10 patients, on average.

SKILLFULLY MANAGED EMERGENT CARE SITUATIONS: Recognized and reacted to emergent patient/resident care situations and intervened while waiting for assistance. Drew on CNA training and experience to accurately recognize need for basic life support, control bleeding, and assist with effective management of behavior crises and other issues.

DEMONSTRATED EFFECTIVE COMMUNICATIONS: Communicated orally with patients/residents, families, the interdisciplinary team, and other support personnel. Served as a preceptor to new nursing assistants (NAs). Assisted with orientation coordination. Assessed practical experience in a clinical setting.

CONSISTENTLY FOLLOWED ESTABLISHED PROTOCOL; MANAGED RECORDS: Removed defective equipment, reported hazards, observed safety regulations, contributed to infection control, and utilized proper aseptic techniques in performance of duties. Ensured strict compliance with established protocols.
Meticulously entered information about residents' conditions in the chart, utilizing appropriate formats. Used the Kiosk for recordkeeping.

EDUCATION / CERTIFICATIONS & LICENSES

Associates of Science, Medical Assisting Science
Keiser University, Fort Lauderdale, FL 33309
Some college coursework completed (30 credit hours as of 10/2020). Degree anticipated: 02/2022

SELECTED COURSEWORK: Introduction to Psychology, Introduction to Computers, General Biology, Advanced Biology, Anatomy & Physiology with Terminology & Disease Process.

CERTIFICATIONS & LICENSES: Certified Nursing Assistant (CNA) / Pennsylvania Registered Nurse Aide, License Number: 99922222. Original Issue Date: 01-02-2007; Expiration Date: 01-01-2022
Basic Life Support (BLS) Certification; CPR Certification

Graduate, Nurse Aide Training Program, 2007
Harrisburg Area Community College (HACC), Harrisburg, PA 11710; Completed a 120-hour program.

ACTIVITY: JOB FAIR SCRIPT

One of the best places to learn about Federal jobs, agencies, and opportunities is at a military career expo. On occasion, the Federal Human Resources Specialist may even bring along a few Direct Hire opportunities for government positions or internships. Have your resume ready to hand out. Your Federal resume should feature your most relevant skills for easy reading and review by the human resources recruiters. Also, practice the job fair script before you go. Prepare your own job fair script here. Practice your script with a friend.

Hello, my name is: ____________________

Where are you from? ____________________

Military service: ____________________

Recent activity: ____________________

What was involved in that? ____________________

What was the result of that activity? ____________________

What was your role? ____________________

What kind of job are you looking for? ____________________

What are your basic skills? ____________________

Where do you want to live? ____________________

LINKEDIN NETWORKING

LinkedIn is THE business channel for recruiting.

However, it is also so much more. LinkedIn provides an opportunity to build a worldwide network of professionals who can assist you with your career. Not only does it work for military to civilian transitions, it also works within the military framework where military to military assignments are concerned.

Many military members have made connections for their next military assignment with another military professional using LinkedIn. LinkedIn can be regarded as a marvelous "networking" tool, though it should not be used as a substitute for good, old-fashioned relationship building.

LinkedIn is a great tool for military spouses for PCS moves. Before LinkedIn, it was very difficult to build a professional network outside of your current assignment. With the worldwide network that LinkedIn provides, military spouses are now able to build a professional network online.

Many of our clients report that their LinkedIn profile was reviewed prior to their interview by the interviewers. The interviewer will have a great impression of you if you have done your work on LinkedIn, and you can research the interviewer prior to your interview.

Suggestions for Using LinkedIn:

- Add an exciting profile to highlight your most outstanding skills.
- Introduce your strengths, mission, and career history to an employer or network.
- Ask for and post recommendations from your best customers or team members who will write about your strengths and accomplishments.
- Post a professional-looking photograph.
- Moving? Put your NEW location into your LinkedIn account.

Did You Know?

Business professionals and human resources managers use LinkedIn to check out potential job candidates. Individuals with more than 20 connections are 34 times more likely to be approached with a job opportunity.

STEP 3
SEARCH USAJOBS

900+	17,609	6 million +	221,979,457
Jobs posted per day	Jobs open per day	Active profiles	Visits per year
The average number of jobs posted per day is 907.	The average number of jobs open per day is 17,609.	USAJOBS has 6,128,845 active profiles to date.	Over the past year, USAJOBS has seen 221,979,457 visits to the site.

Right now, as of this writing, there are over 17,000 vacancy announcements posted on USAJOBS. The process of sifting through that many announcements can be overwhelming, but we will teach you how to narrow down your search and conduct your search efficiently. Also, as you go through this step, we want you to locate a vacancy announcement that you can use as a "target" to aim your resume towards this position. Think about this: every vacancy announcement in USAJOBS will be filled by an individual who targets their resume to the announcement.

Top **USAJOBS Search Tip** for Veterans

 Veterans' Preference applies to U.S. citizen announcements, **NOT Federal employee announcements.**

U.S. Citizen Announcements

With Category Rating (Qualified, Well Qualified, and Best Qualified)—The veteran resume must be "qualified" for veterans' preference to be applied. Non-disabled veterans will rise to the top of the category "they score in (Qualified, Well Qualified, or Best Qualified)." Disabled veterans who are rated qualified will be move to the highest quality category (Best Qualified). All "Best Qualified" applications are forwarded/referred to hiring official for employment consideration.

Federal Employee Announcements

Veterans can apply to these announcements when the announcement is also open to those eligible for Special Appointing Authorities, i.e., VEOA, VRA, 30% Disabled Vet, Schedule A, etc. Veterans' preference (as above) will not be applied to the resumes for this type of announcement. Your resume and questionnaire answers will be reviewed equally along with all applicants.

HOW TO SEARCH USAJOBS

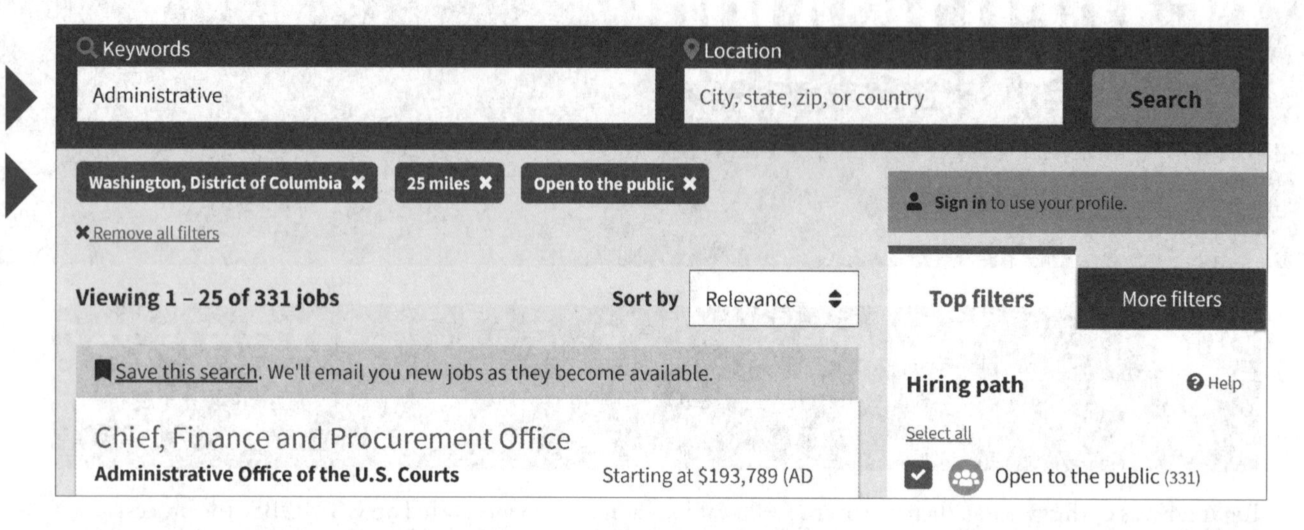

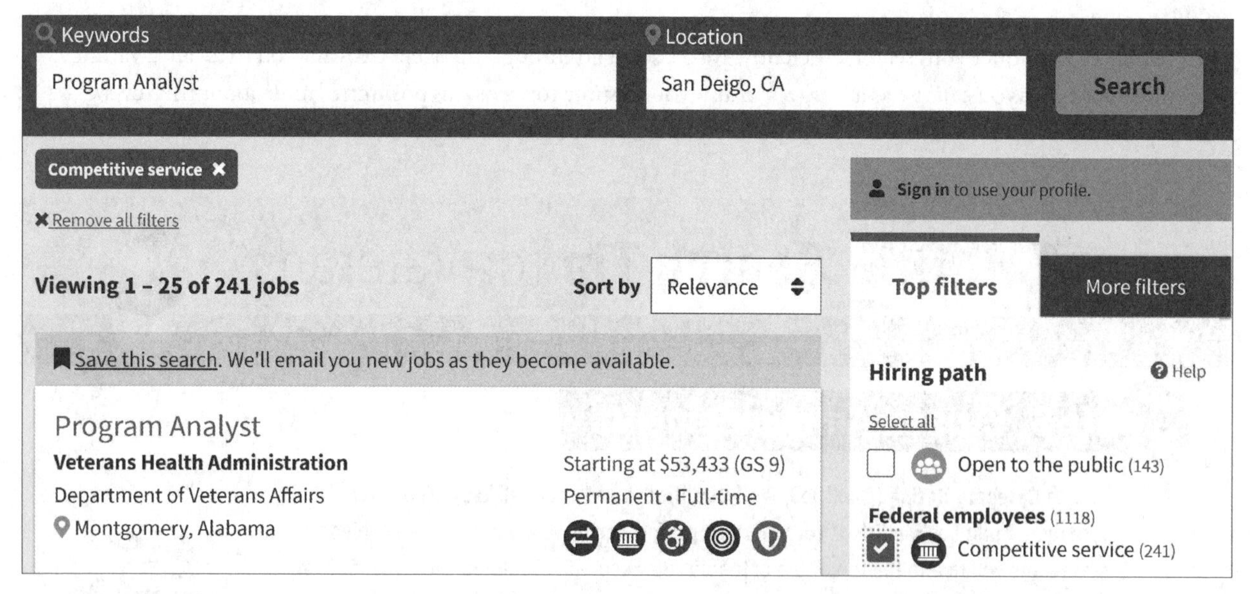

Basic Search

The Basic Search is VERY EASY. This is the easiest search to perform and will return a large number of results.

- Go to *www.usajobs.gov*
- Enter keywords and geographic location.
- Test out using keywords specific to your unique skill set or the correct job title in quotation marks.

FILTER YOUR RESULTS

You can quickly and efficiently refine your USAJOBS vacancy announcement search by using the filters on the righthand side of your search results page. Filter your results based Your Hiring Path!

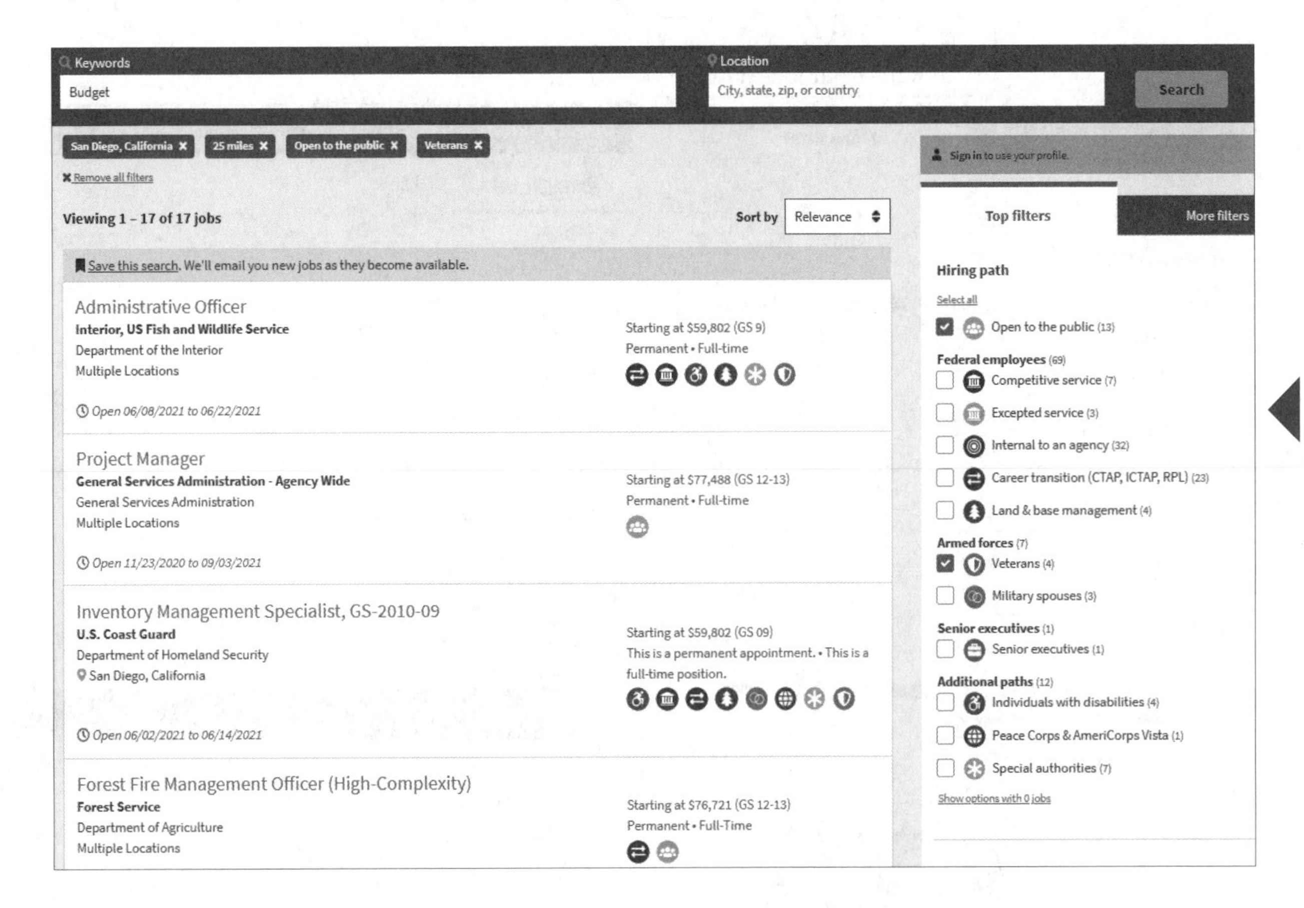

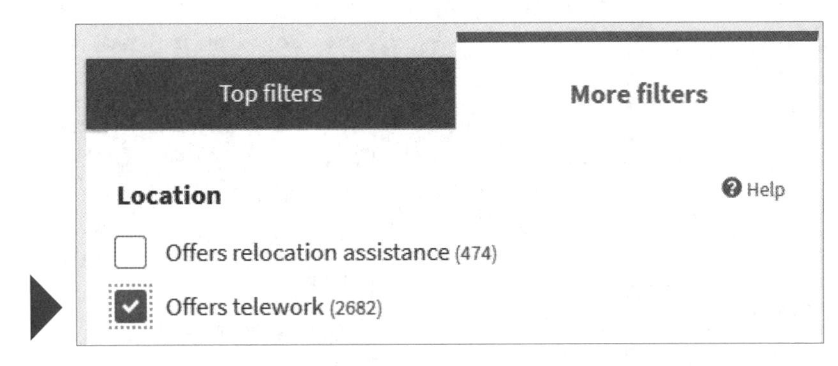

Search for Telework Jobs with the Telework Filter!

MORE FILTERS – GRADE, AGENCY, SERIES

Click on the **More Filters** tab to refine your job search even more. Select your **Grade Level, Agency, and Series!**

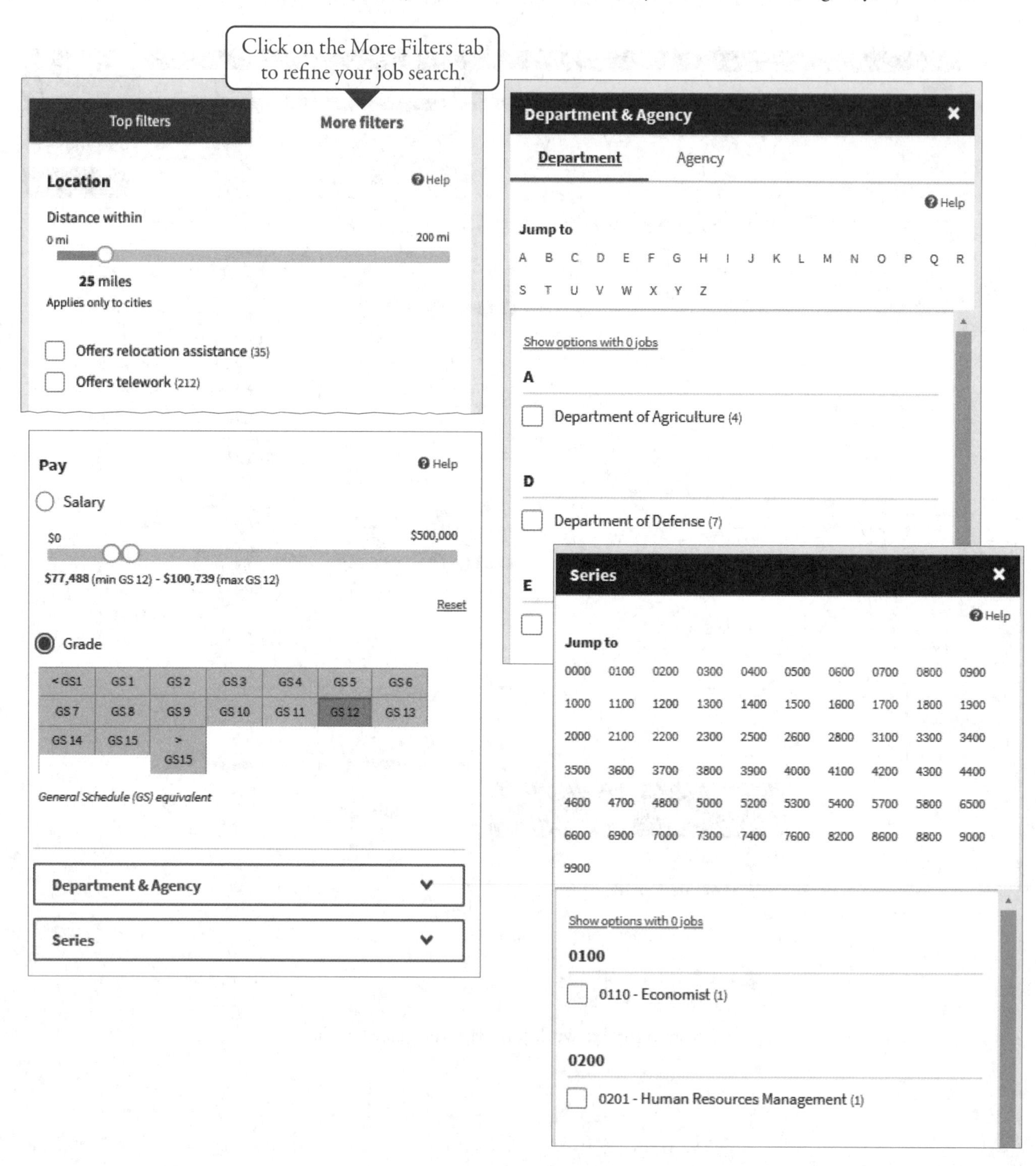

SAVED SEARCHES AND EMAIL NOTIFICATIONS

You can save your searches and get daily emails with your target positions. This is VERY IMPORTANT because many announcements close after they receive 100 applications; or they close after 5 days. If you do not have SAVED SEARCHES, you could miss important job announcements.

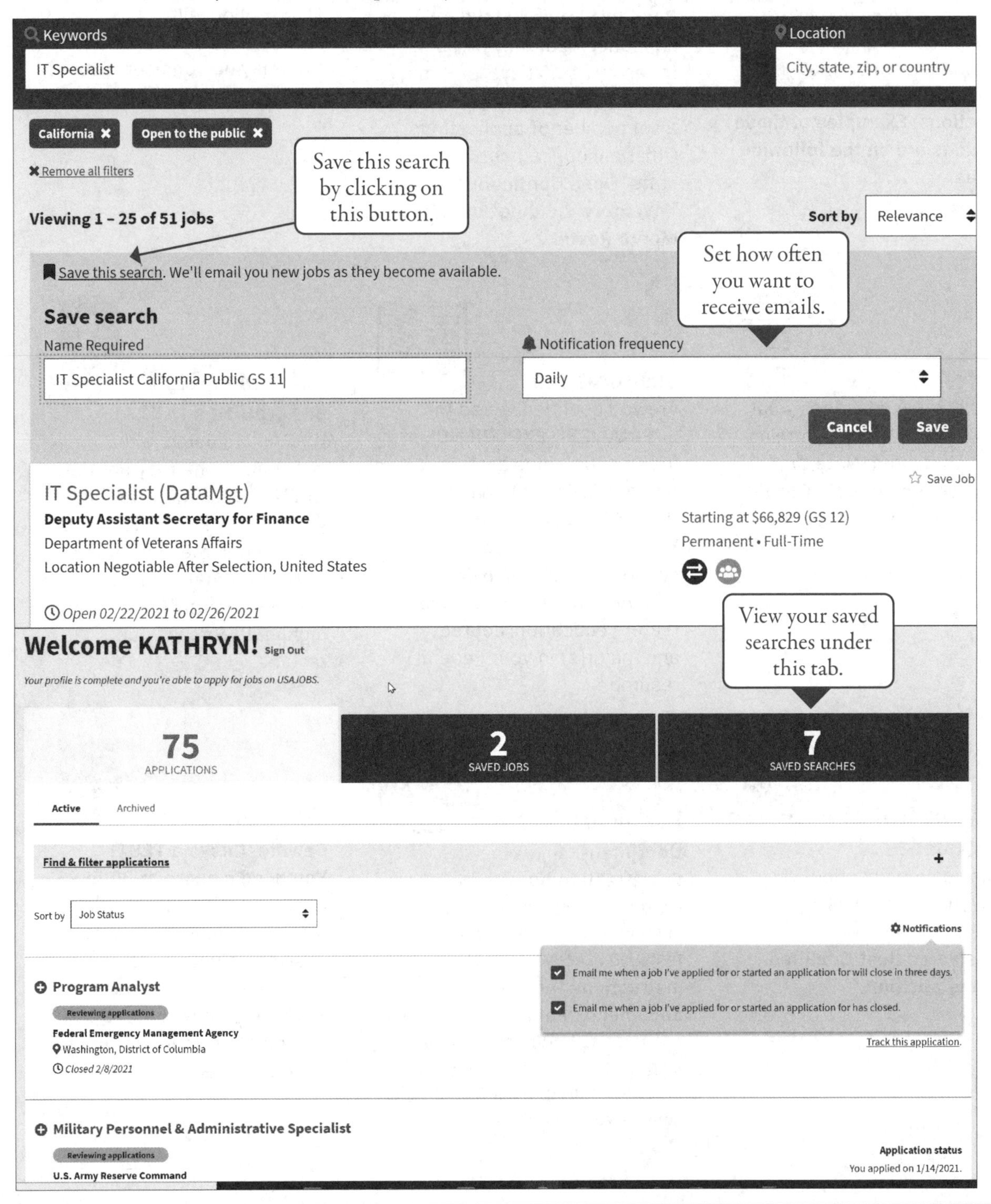

STEP 3

CRITICAL VACANCY ANNOUNCEMENT FEATURES

Follow the Directions!
Be sure to study these sections on every announcement so that you can successfully follow the directions. **Examples of these sections are on the following pages.**

Closing Dates
Read this immediately! An announcement may be open for as few as 5 days, or it may close after an agency receives a set number of applications. Other announcements may state **"Open Continuously," "Inventory Building," or "12 Month Roster."**

Who May Apply?
This section will state the **types of applicants** who may be considered for the position.

Duties
This section describes what tasks you will be performing if you are hired. **Note that this section does NOT have the best keywords for your resume.**

Qualifications
Are you qualified? Read the **SPECIALIZED EXPERIENCE** in the Qualifications section to find out. This section is the **BEST FOR KEYWORDS** for your Federal resume. Also read this section for **EDUCATION REQUIREMENTS**. Be sure to feature education, courses, and major(s) in your Federal resume.

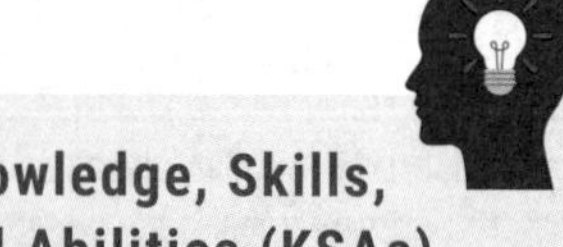

Knowledge, Skills, and Abilities (KSAs)
If KSAs are listed in the announcement, they are the **CRITICAL KEYWORDS** that you will need to cover in your Federal resume. Follow the Outline Format resume examples in this book to highlight KSAs in your resume.

How You Will Be Evaluated
This section describes how the agency will determine who will be considered **Best Qualified for the position.**

How to Apply and Documents
Pay attention here; these instructions are different for each announcement and must be followed exactly. **Read the instructions for required documents.** Pathways Internships and Recent Graduates must upload a copy of transcripts. If hired, you may be required to send an official copy of your transcript.

Questionnaires
Beware, this is a TEST!
You need a score of 90 to 95.
Give yourself all the credit that you can. Reflect your answers in your Federal resume. Human Resources will read your resume to see if it matches your answers to the questions.

SAMPLE VACANCY ANNOUNCEMENT

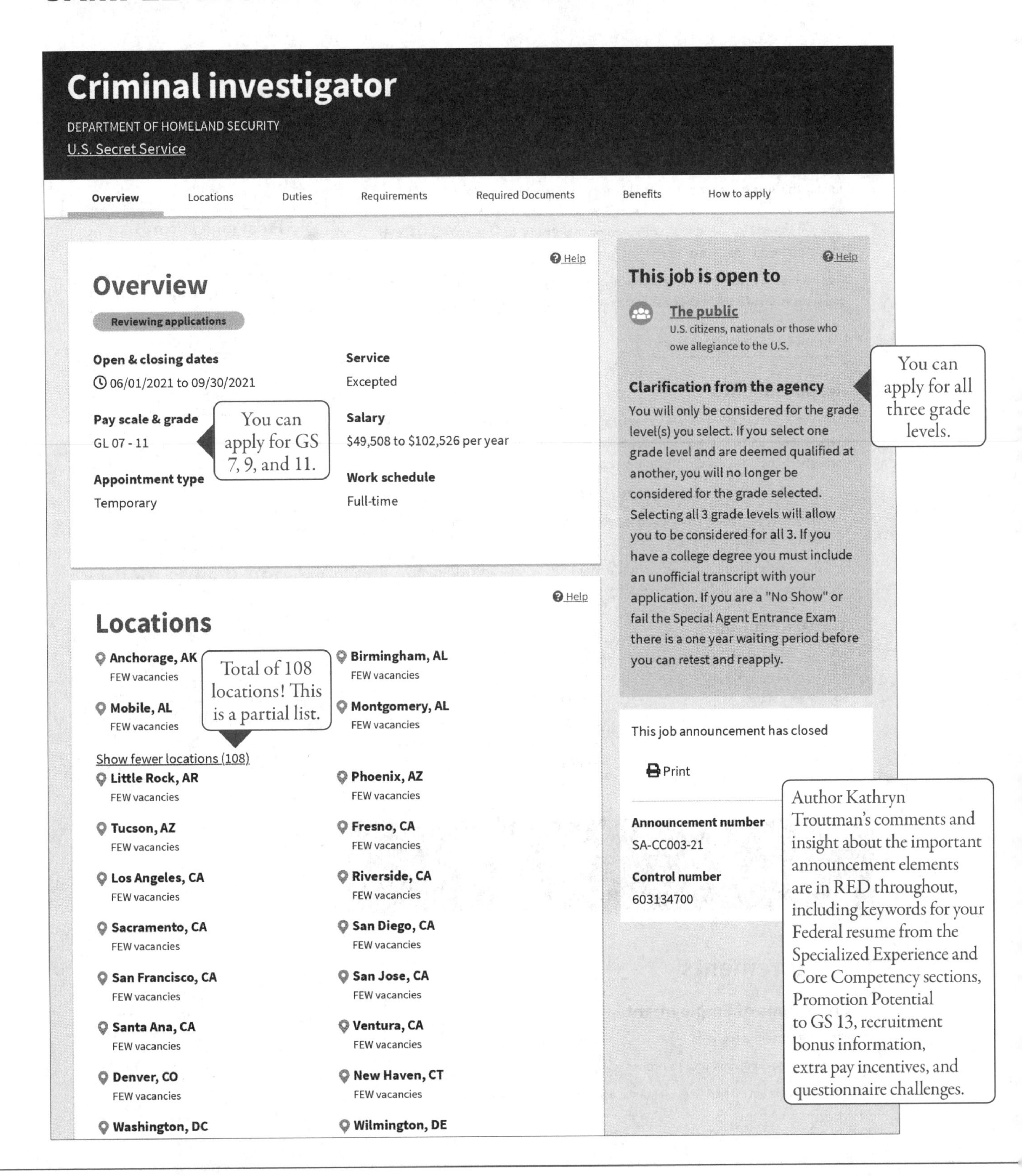

SAMPLE VACANCY ANNOUNCEMENT CONT.

Help

Duties

Summary

Joining the Secret Service as a Special Agent will allow you to perform critical protective and investigative assignments. The special agent position starts at a salary of $49,508 (GL-07, step 1), with promotion potential to $146,120 (GS-13, step 10). For more information on the Secret Service click here.

This position is covered by Law Enforcement Availability Pay (LEAP) and **additional compensation of 25% of the base salary will be added to locality pay.**

Learn more about this agency

Promotion potential to GS 13, Step 10!

25% additional pay in addition to salary and locality pay.

Responsibilities

During the course of their careers, special agents carry out assignments in both investigations and protection and may be assigned to multiple duty stations throughout the U.S. and abroad. Duties include:

Providing protection for various protectees.

Conducting criminal investigations pertaining to financial obligations of the United States.

Planning and implementing security designs for National Special Security Events.

This is short and sweet – three sentences!

Travel Required

Occasional travel - Travel is required 25% or less

Supervisory status

No

Promotion Potential

13 - Full Promotion Potential grade 13 is assigned from the General Schedule (GS) Pay Scale

Career Ladder Position to GS 13

Job family (Series)

1811 Criminal Investigation

Help

Requirements

Conditions of Employment

- U.S. citizenship is required
- Possess a current valid driver's license
- You must obtain a Top Secret Clearance and retain it during your career.

SAMPLE VACANCY ANNOUNCEMENT CONT.

Conditions of Employment you will be required to:

Possess uncorrected visual acuity of no worse than 20/100 binocular, possess corrected visual acuity of 20/20 or better in each eye.(Note: Lasik, ALK, RK, and PRK corrective eye surgeries are acceptable eye surgeries for special agent applicants. Applicants will be considered eligible for the special agent position provided specific visual tests are passed. The following are waiting periods for visual tests: Lasik-2 months after surgery, PRK-6 months after surgery, and ALK and RK-one year after surgery).

Stringent physical requirements!

Hearing loss, as measured by an audiometer, must not exceed 25 decibels (A.S.A. or equivalent I.S.O.) in either ear in the 500,1000, and 2000Hz ranges.

Be at least age 21 at the time of application and less than age 37 at the time you receive a conditional offer of employment, unless you have previous service in a Federal Civilian Law Enforcement position covered by special law enforcement or firefighter retirement provisions, including early or mandatory retirement. Applicants with veteran's preference must receive a conditional offer of employment prior to reaching age 40 to continue in the application process.

Submit to a drug test prior to your appointment and random drug testing while you occupy the position. **Disclose any prior drug use**, attempted use, and/or experimentation.

Carry and use a firearm. Maintaining firearm proficiency is mandatory. You will be ineligible to occupy this position if at any time you have been convicted of a misdemeanor crime of domestic violence, unless you received a pardon or your conviction was expunged or set aside.

Complete 12 weeks of intensive training at the Federal Law Enforcement Training Center(FLETC) in Glynco, GA and 18 weeks of specialized training at the James J. Rowley Training Center in Laurel, MD. Failure to pass the training program on the first attempt may result in separation from the Secret Service. Click here to review standard.

Sign a mobility agreement stating your willingness to accept assignments anywhere within the United States and overseas.

Certify that you have registered with the Selective Service System or are exempt from having to do so, if you are a male applicant born after December 31, 1959.

Be appointed to this position under an **excepted appointment** which is **limited to 3 years and 120 days.** Upon completion of this period, you will either be converted to career status or separated based on the expiration of the appointment.

Qualifications

You are minimally qualified for the GL-07 Level (starting salary $49,508) if you possess one of the following: A bachelor's degree from an accredited college or university with superior academic achievement (S.A.A.) which is based on class standing, grade-point average, or honor society membership (for more information on S.A.A. please click here); **OR** at least one full year of graduate level education (i.e., 18 semester hours); **OR** at least 1 year of specialized experience in, or related to, the

SAMPLE VACANCY ANNOUNCEMENT CONT.

Your resume must show the 1 year of specialized experience OR the education listed.

Qualifications

You are minimally qualified for the GL-07 Level (starting salary $49,508) if you possess one of the following: A bachelor's degree from an accredited college or university with superior academic achievement (S.A.A.) which is based on class standing, grade-point average, or honor society membership (for more information on S.A.A. please click here); **OR** at least one full year of graduate level education (i.e., 18 semester hours); **OR** at least 1 year of specialized experience in, or related to, the investigative methods, protective methods, and law enforcement techniques that provide the specific competencies to successfully perform the position's duties. Experience also includes exercising initiative; attention to detail; judgment in collecting, assembling and developing facts, evidence or other pertinent data; the ability to analyze and evaluate data or evidence to arrive at sound conclusions including applying new information; and the ability to partner with or lead others in the accomplishment of mission activities.

You are minimally qualified for the GL-09 Level (starting salary $55,214) if you possess one of the following: A master's or equivalent graduate degree (such as LL.B. or J.D.) or two full years of progressively higher graduate education, in a related field, leading to such a degree from an accredited college or university; **OR** have at least 1 year of specialized experience equivalent to the GL-7 level such as experience applying law enforcement, protective, or investigative techniques in the performance of job duties; identifying problem areas and proposing and implementing solutions; taking responsibility for own actions and those of team members to ensure the goals and deadlines for the team are met; and leading meeting or seminars on behalf of a professional or academic group; setting work priorities and allocating resources; partnering with other individuals from within and outside the organization; **OR** a combination of specialized experience, as described above, and related graduate level education, beyond the first full year of graduate level study.

KEYWORDS FOR Y OUR FEDERAL RESUME:

- INITIATIVE
- ATTENTION TO DETAIL
- JUDGMENT IN COLLECTING FACTS AND EVIDENCE
- ANALYZE AND EVALUATE DATA
- PARTNER WITH OTHERS TO ACHIEVE MISSION

KEYWORDS FOR YOUR FEDERAL RESUME:

- LAW ENFORCEMENT, PROTECTIVE, OR INVESTIGATIVE TECHNIQUES
- IDENTIFY PROBLEM AREAS AND IMPLEMENT SOLUTIONS
- TEAM MEMBER AND WORK INDEPENDENTLY TO MEET GOALS
- LEAD MEETINGS / PRESENTATIONS
- SET WORK PRIORITIES AND MANAGE RESOURCES
- PARTNER WITH INDIVIDUALS AND EXTERNAL ORGANIZATIONS

SAMPLE VACANCY ANNOUNCEMENT CONT.

You are minimally qualified for the GS-11 Level (Starting salary $64,649) if you possess one of the following: Ph.D. or equivalent doctoral degree, or 3 full years of progressively higher level graduate education leading to such a degree, or LL.M., **OR** have at least 1 year of specialized experience equivalent to the GL-9 level which is defined as experience in, or related to planning and conducting complex criminal investigations to determine violations of Federal laws and regulations; collecting and assembling facts to identify logical conclusion; gathering, analyzing, and evaluating evidence or data; conducting interviews and interrogations; making arrests; conducting searches and seizures; taking responsibility for own actions and those of team members to ensure the goals and deadlines for the team are met; partnering with or leveraging networks or relationships from outside the organization, experience managing complex projects including setting priorities and determining resource requirements; **OR** a combination of specialized experience, as described above, and related graduate level education, beyond the first full year of doctoral level study.

Applicants must successfully complete and pass Phase 1 assessments (see below) to be certified. In addition, applicants must successfully complete and pass Phase II (see below) to receive final consideration for employment.

Phase I:

Credit Check;

Special Agent Entrance Exam (SAEE);

Interview; and

Review Panel (Final Grade and quality category)

Phase II:

Security Interview;

Polygraph examination;

Drug screening;

Medical examination; and

Background investigation (a top secret security clearance)

The Secret Service follows stringent guidelines relating to illegal drug usage. An applicant's history is reviewed and a determination for employment is made according to our guidelines. For more information regarding the U.S. Secret Service drug guidelines please click here. Qualified applicants will only be referred at the highest grade level for which they qualify. Consideration will be given to performance appraisals and incentive awards as an indicator of quality of prior experience.

Education

This job does not have an education qualification requirement.

Additional information

Recruitment incentives may be available depending on an applicant's qualifications. An employee accepting a recruitment incentive must sign a service agreement.

KEYWORDS FOR Y OUR FEDERAL RESUME:

- PLAN AND CONDUCT COMPLEX CRIMINAL INVESTIGATIONS
- ANALYZE AND DETERMINE VIOLATIONS OF FEDERAL LAWS AND REGULATIONS
- COLLECT AND ASSEMBLE FACTS
- CONDUCT INTERVIEWS AND INTERROGATIONS
- MAKE ARRESTS
- CONDUCT SEARCH AND SEIZURES
- ENSURE GOALS AND DEADLINES ARE MET FOR TEAMS
- PARTNER WITH EXTERNAL RELATIONSHIPS
- ESTABLISH PRIORITIES FOR COMPLEX PROJECTS

You can qualify with Experience Only for this position.

You can write a Superior Qualifications Letter and ask for a 25% sign-on bonus to begin.

SAMPLE VACANCY ANNOUNCEMENT CONT.

How You Will Be Evaluated

You will be evaluated for this job based on how well you meet the qualifications above.

We will review your resume and supporting documentation to ensure you meet the minimum qualification requirements. If you meet the minimum qualifications, your resume and occupational questionnaire will be submitted to a review panel wherein you will be placed in one of three categories, Qualified, Well Qualified, and Best Qualified, based on your experience, education, training and competencies. You will receive a conditional job offer if you are determined Well Qualified or Best Qualified for a grade level by the panel.

You will only receive consideration for the grade level(s) for which you applied, i.e., if you only applied to the GS-11, but the review panel determined you are Best Qualified for the GL-9, you will not receive further consideration for this position. **You are encouraged to apply for all 3 grade levels to maximize your consideration for this position.**

The competencies or knowledge, skills, and abilities needed to perform this job are:

> Ability to display a high standard of ethical conduct and can be trusted in all work situations; chooses an ethical course of action and does the right thing, even in the face of opposition; encourages others to behave accordingly.
>
> Ability to deal calmly and effectively with high stress or dangerous situations; remains calm, even-tempered, and in control of emotions, as appropriate for the situation.
>
> Skill in demonstrating good judgment by making sound, timely and well-informed decisions without deferring actions when decisions need to be made; considers the impact and implications of decisions; commits to action and follows through on decisions.
>
> Ability to identify problems, determine underlying issues and potential causes and generate and evaluate alternatives to arrive at and implement an effective solution.
>
> Ability to demonstrate fairness, professionalism and tact when interacting with others; understands and interacts effectively with a variety of people to include those who are difficult, hostile, or distressed; adjusts interpersonal style, as needed, to interact with differing individuals.

Veterans who have a compensable service-connected disability of at least 10% are listed in the best qualified category. Other 10-point preference eligibles and veterans with 5-point preference who meet the eligibility and qualification requirements are placed above non-preference eligibles within the category in which they qualify.

Your on-line application will be rated on the extent, quality, and relevance of the following: your experience, education and training, and competencies. All applicants are evaluated on competencies related to law enforcement methods and techniques, protective methods and techniques, investigative methods and techniques, initiative, problem solving, attention to detail, learning, partnering, planning and organizing, and leadership. Candidates will be rated as Qualified, Well Qualified, and Best Qualified upon completion of Phase I assessments. All answers in the online process must be substantiated by your resume. Upon review, your

These competencies are critical to cover in your Work History.

KEYWORDS:

ETHICAL STANDARDS

DEMONSTRATE CALM REACTION IN STRESSFUL SITUATIONS

DEMONSTRATE GOOD JUDGMENT AND DECISIVENESS

ABLE TO IDENTIFY PROBLEMS AND ISSUES AND GIVE ALTERNATIVES FOR SOLUTIONS

DEMONSTRATE FAIRNESS WHEN INTERACTING WITH OTHERS

This announcement will apply **Veterans' Preference**.

The online application is amazing... more than 104 job-related questions. Stay calm, patient, and answer the questions! The questions will cover the competencies underlined here.

SAMPLE VACANCY ANNOUNCEMENT CONT.

Help

How to Apply

This position is being advertised via SecretService Hire which is an automated staffing system. To begin your online application, click the Apply Online button and follow the prompts to register or sign into USAJOBS, complete the online questionnaire, and submit the required documents. See Required Documents section for more detail. You must complete the application process and submit any required documents by 11:59 p.m. Eastern Standard Time (EST) on the closing date of this announcement.

If you cannot apply online, you may contact the Talent and Employee Acquisition Management Division, Special Agent Support Branch at sasupport@usss.dhs.gov OR by calling (202) 406-5271 between the hours of 9:00 am and 5:30 pm EST (excluding Federal holidays) prior to the closing date of this announcement to receive assistance. The Secret Service provides reasonable accommodation to applicants with disabilities, on a case-by-case basis.

Even though USSS uses an automated staffing system, human resources specialists will read your resumes!

Close

Agency contact information

TAD

Phone
202-406-5271

Fax
999-999-9999

Email
sasupport@usss.dhs.gov

Address
United States Secret Service (DHS-USSS)
Please read entire announcement
Please apply online
Washington, District of Columbia 20223
United States

Learn more about this agency

Next steps

Applicants who receive a passing score on the SAEE or structured interview may retain and use the score indefinitely unless significant changes are made to the test, at which point applicants who reapply for a vacancy must retest on the newest version of the assessments. Applicants who have taken but did not pass the assessments must wait one year (12 months) before retesting and to reapply for this position.

You may check the status of your application for this position by going to www.usajobs.gov. Click on the "My USAJOBS" tab, enter your user ID and password, and click on "My Applications". You will also receive an e-mail notification regarding your application status. For more information on applying for Federal employment, please click here.

Check your results in My Applications on USAJOBS.

SAMPLE VACANCY ANNOUNCEMENT QUESTIONNAIRE

The online questionnaire had 104 questions that were job-related. Get a cup of tea, relax, and answer the questions! Twenty questions are skill-related; the other questions are medical, eligibility, and security questions.

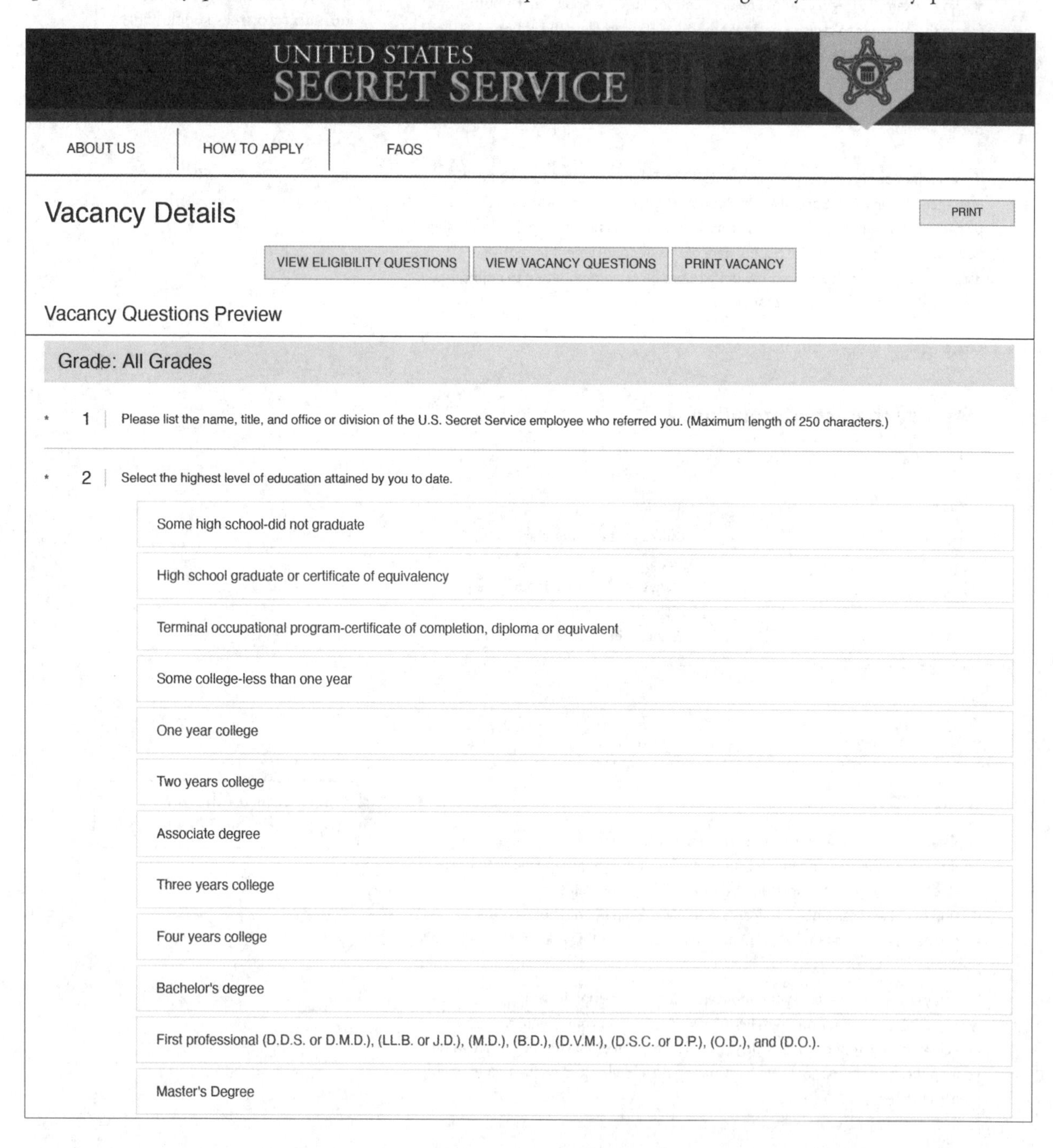
UNITED STATES
SECRET SERVICE

ABOUT US | HOW TO APPLY | FAQS

Vacancy Details

PRINT

VIEW ELIGIBILITY QUESTIONS | VIEW VACANCY QUESTIONS | PRINT VACANCY

Vacancy Questions Preview

Grade: All Grades

* 1 | Please list the name, title, and office or division of the U.S. Secret Service employee who referred you. (Maximum length of 250 characters.)

* 2 | Select the highest level of education attained by you to date.

- Some high school-did not graduate
- High school graduate or certificate of equivalency
- Terminal occupational program-certificate of completion, diploma or equivalent
- Some college-less than one year
- One year college
- Two years college
- Associate degree
- Three years college
- Four years college
- Bachelor's degree
- First professional (D.D.S. or D.M.D.), (LL.B. or J.D.), (M.D.), (B.D.), (D.V.M.), (D.S.C. or D.P.), (O.D.), and (D.O.).
- Master's Degree

STEP 4
FIND KEYWORDS

Keywords are critical to the success of your Federal resume. You need to find the keywords in order to target your resume to a particular vacancy announcement.

How Many Keywords Do I Need?

Find at least **5 to 7 keywords** and keyword phrases. However, the more keywords you can include to help translate your experience into terms that the Human Resources Specialist can clearly identify, the greater your chances of having the HR Specialist understand how your qualifications match the desired qualifications in the vacancy announcement.

Training Administrator

DEPARTMENT OF THE HOMELAND SECURITY

Federal Law Enforcement Training Centers

Specialized Experience For the GS-12 grade level:

You qualify for the GS-12 grade level if you possess one of the following:

One year of specialized experience equivalent to the GS-11 grade level in the federal service providing educational/training consultation, program administration, registration, program analytics/diagnostics, and recommendations in support of the evaluation and revision of educational and/or training program curricula related to law enforcement training programs.

ACTIVITY: Keywords from Training Administrator Position

From the vacancy announcement on the previous pages, find and list 5 to 7 keywords:

4 PLACES TO FIND KEYWORDS IN VACANCY ANNOUNCEMENTS

Contact Representative/Collection Representative (English and Bilingual)

DEPARTMENT OF THE TREASURY
Internal Revenue Service

Overview | Locations | Duties | Requirements | Required Documents | Benefits | How to apply

Overview

Help

Accepting applications

Open & closing dates
06/28/2021 to 06/24/2022

Service
Competitive

Pay scale & grade
GS 5

Salary
$35,265 to $55,925 per year

Appointment type
Multiple Appointment Types

Work schedule
Full-time

This job is open to

Help

Career transition (CTAP, ICTAP, RPL)
Federal employees who meet the definition of a "surplus" or "displaced" employee.

The public
U.S. citizens, nationals or those who owe allegiance to the U.S.

Clarification from the agency
Open to U.S. Citizens/Nationals

More than 5,000 jobs are advertised with one job announcement!

Locations

Help

5482 vacancies in the following locations:

- Fresno, CA
- Oakland, CA
- Denver, CO
- Jacksonville, FL

Show fewer locations (24)

- Chamblee, GA
- West Des Moines, IA
- Indianapolis, IN
- Covington, KY
- Andover, MA
- Baltimore, MD
- Detroit, MI
- Kansas City, MO
- Saint Louis, MO
- Cheektowaga, NY
- Holtsville, NY
- Cleveland, OH
- Portland, OR
- Philadelphia, PA
- Pittsburgh, PA
- Guaynabo, PR
- San Juan, PR
- Franklin, TN

Apply

Print | Share | Save

Announcement number
21-11156094K-SBWIX-962-5T8

Control number
605956800

Author Kathryn Troutman provides insight about the important announcement sections and mandatory keywords and core competencies that you will need to cover in your Work History or Education to match the announcement qualifications. This is important so you can get BEST QUALIFIED!

1. Duties and Responsibilities—Learn about the Job

Duties

Summary

Click on "Learn more about this agency" button below to view **Eligibilities** being considered and other **IMPORTANT** information.

WHERE CAN I FIND OUT MORE ABOUT OTHER IRS CAREERS? Visit us on the web at www.jobs.irs.gov

Learn more about this agency

Responsibilities

WHAT IS THE WAGE & INVESTMENT (W&I) and SMALL BUSINESS/SELF EMPLOYED (SBSE)DIVISION?
A description of the business units can be found at:
https://www.jobs.irs.gov/about/who/business-divisions

The following are the duties of this position at the full working level. If you are selected at a lower grade level, you will have the opportunity to learn to perform these duties and will receive training to help you grow in this position.

Uses sophisticated interviewing techniques, the employee reviews individual circumstances and goals, and advises on the most advantageous ways to meet them.

Elicits sensitive, personal and financial information, e.g., innocent spouse determinations, bankruptcies, or draws out information the individual may attempt to withhold, e.g., additional sources of income, overpayments, to ensure compliance with reporting and disclosure requirements.

Makes determinations and uses sound judgment concerning controversial matters in reporting as appropriate the degree to which the individual understood their responsibilities and whether errors in their records reflected honest mistakes or fraudulent intent.

Develops, analyzes and evaluates information involving the research of records and the nature of each inquiry including the way it was presented in order to inform and advise, answer inquiries, or resolve problems related to the unique circumstances of each individual or fulfill regulatory requirements.

Explains what future actions are necessary to achieve voluntary compliance by computing and/or advising on tax liability and probable assessment of taxes in cases involving: varied sources of income, including self-employment, itemized personal and business expense deductions, or carryover/carry back of capital losses and investment credit from prior years, or comparable issues requiring reference to the tax code and precedent.

Travel Required

Occasional travel - You may be expected to travel for this position.

Supervisory status	Promotion Potential
No	8

You do not have to prove all of this in your Federal resume. This is the description of the job, if you are hired.

This great to see. The position has Promotion Potential to GS 8!

2. Requirements – Specialized Experience

Qualifications

Federal experience is not required. The experience may have been gained in the public sector, private sector or Volunteer Service. One year of experience refers to full-time work; part-timework is considered on a prorated basis. To ensure full credit for your work experience, please indicate dates of employment by month/year, and indicate number of hours worked per week, on your resume.

You must meet the following requirements by the closing date of this announcement:

GS-05 Level:

SPECIALIZED EXPERIENCE: You must have one year of specialized experience at a level of difficulty and responsibility equivalent to the GS-04 grade level in the Federal service. Specialized experience for this position includes: experience that may have been gained in work with records, documents or financial accounts which involved applying established rules and procedures, or experience gained through work in positions that involved frequent contact with the public researching and responding to non-routine requests for information orally or in writing. The following are examples of specialized experience that may be qualifying and are not all inclusive:

Applying laws, rules or regulations and written guidelines;

Conducting face to face and/or telephone interviews (e.g., collection agency, telemarketing, customer service, sales) resolving problems and issues;

Negotiating with others to resolve issues;

Performing administrative and technical procedures using a computer to locate and review records and reconcile discrepancies;

Working with records or financial accounts applying established rules and procedures (e.g., basic accounting, credits and debits, researching and/or adjusting accounts).

OR

EDUCATION: You may substitute education for specialized experience as follows: Completed at least 4 years of education above the high school level leading to a Bachelor's degree (120 semester hours, 180 quarter hours or 2880 formal classroom hours) or a Bachelors or higher degree.

OR

COMBINATION OF EXPERIENCE AND EDUCATION: You may qualify by a combination of experience and education. Options for qualifying based on a combination will be identified in the online questions.

AND

You must meet the following special requirements:

BILINGUAL POSITIONS ONLY: We are filling both English and bilingual vacancies. For the bilingual vacancies, applicants will be required to self-certify proficiency in

Volunteer experience can be used to demonstrate qualifications for the position. You would need to create a "job block" to show the required information.

This is the "pot of gold" for keywords to match in your Federal resume Work History section. See the sample in this Step and find the keywords in the Outline Format – she was SELECTED!

The underlined words are keywords that you should feature in your Federal resume in the Outline Format!

3. How You Will Be Evaluated

How You Will Be Evaluated

You will be evaluated for this job based on how well you meet the qualifications above.

Your application includes your resume, responses to the online questions, and required supporting documents. Please be sure that your resume includes detailed information to support your qualifications for this position; failure to provide sufficient evidence in your resume may result in a "not qualified" determination.

Rating: You will be assessed on the following competencies (knowledge, skills, abilities, and other characteristics):

Arithmetic/Mathematical Reasoning

Attention to Detail

Conscientiousness

Emotional Intelligence

Independence

Interpersonal Skills

Persistence

Planning and Organizing

Reading

Self-Esteem

Writing

Pot of Gold – for Keywords and Competencies for your Resume, the Assessment Questionnaire, and the Interview.

This Contact Representative position involves a lot of interviews, document review, and problem-solving. The competencies listed here are REAL. Demonstrate these in your resume the best you can with examples of your documentation and customer services duties and responsibilities.

4. Self-Assessment Questionnaire

Below are Sample Questions from the Questionnaire that demonstrate the Competencies for the job! There are 34 questions in this Questionnaire. The work scenarios are very interesting. Choose the answer that seems the most reasonable for the position.

Position Title	Contact Representative/Collection Representative (English and Bilingual)
Agency	Internal Revenue Service
Announcement Number	21-11156094K-SBWIX-962-5T8
Open Period	Monday, June 28, 2021 to Friday, June 24, 2022

22. While staffing the taxpayer hotline, you receive a call from a taxpayer who has not yet received his expected tax refund. He states that without the refund, he will not be able to pay his bills or put food on the table. While explaining to you why the refund is so important, the taxpayer states that he should just "end it."

Given this situation, what would you **most** likely do?

- A. Get the accurate information about the refund status to the taxpayer once you are able to identify its status.
- B. Show empathy to the taxpayer about his feelings and assure him that it will work out.
- C. Immediately assure the taxpayer that the refund will be deposited soon even before checking its true status.
- D. Show empathy to the taxpayer but instant message your manager to alert him of the emergency.
- E. None of the above

Refer back to the DUTIES section to review the job!

MATCH YOUR RESUME TO THE KEYWORDS FOR CONTACT REPRESENTATIVE

APPLY GUIDANCE AND REGULATIONS
INTERVIEW SKILLS – TELEPHONE OR FACE-TO-FACE
CUSTOMER SERVICES
NEGOTIATE TO RESOLVE PROBLEMS
COMPUTER SKILLS AND COMPUTER RESEARCH
REVIEW DOCUMENTS AND FINANCIAL ACCOUNTS

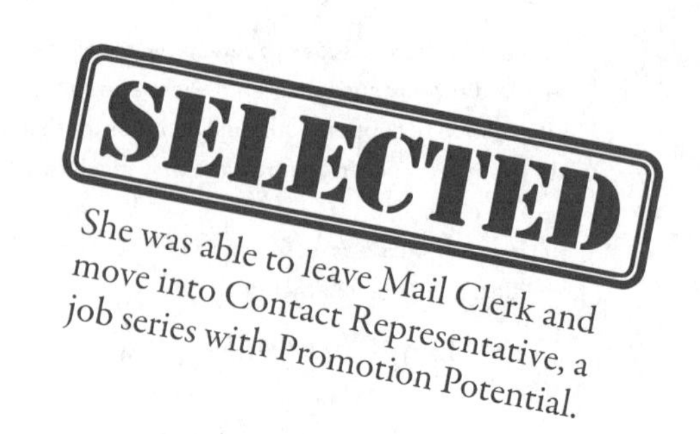

WORK EXPERIENCE:

Mail Clerk **Veterans Affairs** **Salisbury, NC 28144**	**April 2019-Present** **GS-05** **40 Hours/week**

At the Veterans Affairs Office, we work with 300 veterans per month. In my position, I provide secretarial and administrative support to a variety of customers.

CUSTOMER SERVICES: Communicate effectively and professionally with staff at varying grade levels. Answer office phone calls and provide answers to callers, locating and communicating necessary information. When necessary, direct caller to the proper department/person to provide needed information.

INTERVIEW SKILLS: Assist veterans with signing in on the kiosk, making sure that they are in the right area for appointments. Provide excellent customer service and efficiently resolve problems at the lowest level. Receive phone calls for veterans and contractors.

APPLY KNOWLEDGE OF GUIDANCE AND REGULATIONS: Receive and handle hazardous and/or perishable materials, urgent, confidential, and sensitive documents (Express Mail, Priority Mail), and provide signature acknowledging receipt when required. Order supplies for distribution to entire hospital and shipment to other facilities.

PROBLEM-SOLVING AND REVIEW MEDICAL AND FINANCIAL DOCUMENTS: Manage daily independent operation and security of a variety of mail handling equipment, such as a mail meter, sorter, folder, or scale. Maintain the privacy, confidentiality, and security of patients' medical records and employee data. Problem-solve based on existing organization guidelines.

COMPUTER SKILLS AND COMPUTER RESEARCH: Use Talent Management System (TMS) several times a week for training and certification. Track employees' TMS records. Manage records and regulations, including maintaining and disposing of the records. Assess all outgoing mail for proper and complete addressing, proper labeling, and packaging.

KEY ACCOMPLISHMENTS

- **Problem Solving:** On one occasion, we had a massive mailout when one of the mailroom machines began malfunctioning. The malfunction also meant that some of the mailings had to be re-printed. I fixed the machine and stayed overtime to complete the mailing which went out the next morning. I received employee of the month.

STEP 5
EXPLORE YOUR CORE COMPETENCIES

Core Competencies were "soft skills," but now USAJOBS announcements are adding core competencies which represent skills required for the position. These are not just "soft skills." In fact, these core competencies can be the HEADLINES for work history paragraphs in the Outline Format. These core competencies represent the important competencies needed for the job. Cover these core competencies in your Federal resume!

Management and Program Analyst

Department of Energy

OFFICE OF INTELLIGENCE AND COUNTERINTELLIGENCE

Overview

Accepting Applications

Open & closing dates
08/26/2021 to 09/07/2021

Service
Excepted

Pay scale & grade
GS 12 - 13

Salary
$87,198 to $134,798 per year

Appointment type
Permanent

Work schedule
Full-time

Summary

This position is the Executive Assistant to the Principal Deputy Director with responsibilities for coordinating initial tasking and consolidation of inputs to complex analytical issues, to ensure that senior management are informed and briefed accordingly.

How You Will Be Evaluated

Your qualifications will be evaluated on the following competencies (knowledge, skills, abilities and other characteristics):

- ADMINISTRATION AND MANAGEMENT
- DATABASE ADMINISTRATION
- ORGANIZATIONAL DEVELOPMENT
- PROBLEM SOLVING

CORE COMPETENCIES: PEER SPECIALIST

Peer Specialist

DEPARTMENT OF VETERANS AFFAIRS

Veterans Health Administration

Overview

Accepting Applications

Open & closing dates
08/23/2021 to 09/13/2021

This job will close when we have reached **50 applications** which may be sooner than the closing date. Learn more

Service
Competitive

Pay scale & grade
GS 7 - 9

Salary
$37,674 to $59,907 per year

Duties

Summary

The position functions as an interdisciplinary team member, assisting physicians and other professional/ non-professional personnel in a rehabilitation treatment program. Peer specialists perform a variety of therapeutic and supportive tasks that include assisting Veterans in articulating their goals for recovery, learning and practicing new skills, helping them monitor their progress, assisting them in their treatment.

You will be rated on the following competencies for this position:

- COMMUNICATIONS
- CONFLICT MANAGEMENT
- CUSTOMER SERVICE
- INTERPERSONAL SKILLS
- TECHNICAL COMPETENCE

CORE COMPETENCIES: QUALITY ASSURANCE SPECIALIST

Quality Assurance Specialist

DEPARTMENT OF NAVY

United States Fleet Forces Command

Overview

Accepting Applications

Open & closing dates
08/30/2021 to 09/03/2021

Service
Competitive

Pay scale & grade
GS 11 - 12

Salary
$77,488 to $100,739 per year

Appointment type
Permanent

Work schedule
Full-time

Summary

You will serve as a QUALITY ASSURANCE SPECIALIST in the QUALITY ASSURANCE DEPARTMENT, CONTRACT ADMINISTRATION QUALITY ASSURANCE PROGRAM SUPPORT DIVISION of SOUTHEAST REG MAINTENANCE CTR SERMC.

How You Will Be Evaluated

When the application process is complete, we will review your resume to ensure you meet the hiring eligibility and qualification requirements listed in this announcement. You will be rated based on the information provided in your resume and responses to the Occupational Questionnaire, along with your supporting documentation to determine your ability to demonstrate the following competencies:

- INSPECTION MANAGEMENT
- ORAL COMMUNICATION
- QUALITY ASSURANCE
- RISK ASSESSMENT
- WRITTEN COMMUNICATION

CORE COMPETENCIES: FACILITIES SPECIALIST

Facilities Specialist

DEPARTMENT OF ARMY

U.S. Army Corp of Engineers

Logistics Activity

Overview

Accepting Applications

Open & closing dates
09/02/2021 to 09/09/2021

Service
Competitive

Pay scale & grade
GS 9

Salary
$58,083 to $75,507 per year

Appointment type
Permanent

Work schedule
Full-time

Summary

About the Position: The Facilities Specialist serves as primary point of contact for all facilities, space and building management functions of a supported USACE Divisional Headquarters Building. The secondary focus of this position is oversight of vehicle fleet and supply management activities.

How You Will Be Evaluated

You will be evaluated on the basis of your level of competency in the following areas:

- FACILITIES OPERATIONS MANAGEMENT
- PROGRAM/PROJECT MANAGEMENT
- SAFETY, SECURITY, AND FIRE PROTECTION

CORE COMPETENCIES: CONTRACT ADMINISTRATOR

Contract Administrator

DEPARTMENT OF DEFENSE

Defense Contract Management Agency

DCMA West (P8)

Overview

Accepting Applications

Open & closing dates
08/30/2021 to 09/03/2021

Service
Competitive

Pay scale & grade
GS 9 - 11

Salary
$61,019 to $95,980 per year

Appointment type
Permanent

Work schedule
Full-time

Responsibilities

- If selected at the GS-09 level, duties will be performed in a developmental capacity.
- Serves as a Contract Administrator assigned to a team that administers government contracts/grants/agreements for one or more contractors
- Incumbent is assigned a group of contract/grants/agreements for which the employee performs the full range of contract functions up to the point of signature, including contract administration and contract closeout.

How You Will Be Evaluated

You will be evaluated for this job on how well you meet the qualifications above.
The assessments for this job will measure the following Competencies :

- CONTRACT PERFORMANCE MANAGEMENT
- INITIATION OF WORK
- TERMS AND CONDITIONS

SENIOR EXECUTIVE SERVICE CORE COMPETENCIES

Office of Personnel Management, Senior Executive Service (SES)
EXECUTIVE CORE QUALIFICATIONS (ECQS)

Leading Change

This core qualification involves the ability to bring about strategic change, both within and outside the organization, to meet organizational goals. Inherent to this ECQ is the ability to establish an organizational vision and to implement it in a continuously changing environment.

Leading People

This core qualification involves the ability to lead people toward meeting the organization's vision, mission, and goals. Inherent to this ECQ is the ability to provide an inclusive workplace that fosters the development of others, facilitates cooperation and teamwork, and supports constructive resolution of conflicts.

Results Driven

This core qualification involves the ability to meet organizational goals and customer expectations. Inherent to this ECQ is the ability to make decisions that produce high-quality results by applying technical knowledge, analyzing problems, and calculating risks.

Business Acumen

This core qualification involves the ability to manage human, financial, and information resources strategically.

Building Coalitions

This core qualification involves the ability to build coalitions internally and with other federal agencies, state and local governments, nonprofit and private sector organizations, foreign governments, or international organizations to achieve common goals.

Competencies

Leading Change	Leading People	Results Driven	Business Acumen	Building Coalitions
Creativity & Innovation	Conflict Management	Accountability	Financial Management	Partnering
External Awareness	Leveraging Diversity	Customer Service	Human Capital Management	Political Savvy
Flexibility	Developing Others	Decisiveness	Technology Management	Influencing/ Negotiating
Resilience	Team Building	Entrepreneurship		
Strategic Thinking		Problem Solving		
Vision		Technical Credibility		

STEP 6

WRITE YOUR FEDERAL RESUME

A Federal Resume Is **NOT** a ...

... Private Industry Resume

WHY: Too short. Not enough info.

... Bulleted Resume

WHY: This format is usually just another version of the Private Industry resume. Even with bullets, it is still too short and does not have enough detail.

... Big Block Resume

WHY: Have you tried to actually read one of these lately? It's nearly impossible!

... Functional Resume

WHY: You must list your most recent employment first, not last.

If you ever receive a message like the one below in response to an application, it is time to fix your Federal resume format!

Your resume did not document either the number of hours worked per week for all jobs listed, a detailed description of your duties performed, or the month/year to month/year worked for all jobs listed, as required by the vacancy announcement. Please be sure to read each announcement for complete qualification requirements and instructions on 'How to Apply.'

A **Competitive** Federal Resume ...

Is 3 to 5 Pages in Length

WHY: The Federal resume must include certain information in order for you to be rated as Best Qualified for a position. Each generalized and specialized skill that you have developed in your career has to be written into the document.

Matches the Job Announcement

WHY: To be successful, the Federal resume must match the job announcement by making sure KEYWORDS are very easy to find and showing how you have the Knowledge, Skills, and Abilities for the job, including those listed in the Questionnaire, which is Part 2 of the Federal job application.

Includes Accomplishments

WHY: In order to be rated Best Qualified, you must include accomplishments that will prove the Knowledge, Skills, and Abilities or Specialized Experience in the announcement. This information will prove your Past Performance and help you get REFERRED to a supervisor.

Lists Employment in Reverse Chronological Order

WHY: This order is used by the resume builder in USAJOBS.gov.

Includes Information Required in Your Federal Resume

The Federal resume **must match** the USAJOBS Resume Builder fields. We recommend that you use the USAJOBS Resume Builder to create your resume for the first time.

And last but not least...
USES THE OUTLINE FORMAT!

OUTLINE FORMAT FEDERAL RESUME

The Outline Format Federal Resume was created by Kathryn Troutman in 1996 for the first edition of the *Federal Resume Guidebook*. It is the preferred resume format for HR Specialists, who say that the format makes it easy to see the applicant's qualifications for a position. It is also used by a number of agencies as the recommended format. The following example provides an introduction into how a single job block written in the Outline Format should look.

VETERAN COMMUNITY ENGAGEMENT/ PROJECT MANAGEMENT
Vice President, Native American Women Warriors 11/2016 to 4/2020
P.O. Box 8145, Pueblo, CO 81008 40 hours per week
Supervisor: Enola Jones, 777-555-8888, may contact

Mission: A 501(c)(3) Non-Profit Organization to assist Native American women veterans in receiving help and tools to empower themselves; to take on modern challenges in education and employment; and to guide those needing special services.

DEVELOPED GOALS: Developed the organization by-laws to submit for non-profit designation. Developed partnership with veteran and community organizations, businesses, Tribes, federal and local governments to provide project consultation, social, economic, and health training.

Paragraphs, not bullets

SENIOR ADVISOR: Provided advice on organizational mission and goals. Recommended strategic planning conference to establish the organization systems and processes.

DESIGNED OPERATIONAL PLANS: Attended strategic planning conference hosted by Native Strategies. Developed an organization operation plan to stand up Native American Women Warriors. The plan assisted the leadership team to organize, create, develop, and implement processes and standard operating procedures. Created database to partner with other organizations.

ALL CAPS headlines for each paragraph using KEYWORDS from the announcement

DESIGNED SYSTEMS AND DATA TO EVALUATE PROGRAMS: Created after-action reports, interviews, and surveys after every event to measure the effectiveness of the event and to determine if the organization is being run as intended and reaching its intended audience.

WROTE AND EDITED MEMORANDUMS AND REPORTS: Wrote 24 after-action reports upon completing events or projects. These reports were formulated from members input. Created and completed financial reports. Reviewed and edited standard operating procedures and agreements for the organization president.

KEY ACCOMPLISHMENTS:

- FORMULATED POLICIES TO IMPROVE WOMEN'S INITIATIVES: Invited to meet with congressional leaders in Washington, DC, which resulted in creation of a women's mentorship program for the military members on active duty. Members met with the Veterans Affairs Office of Tribal Governmental Affairs for a briefing on current status of issues regarding Tribal veterans' access to Veterans Affairs Healthcare and benefits. An after-action report was written and submitted to congressional leaders for action.
- Managed attendance at the NYC Veterans Day parade in 2018 and 2019, San Diego Veterans Day Parade in 2018, and Inaugural Parade in 2016. These projects were a major undertaking by the organization with wide variety of tasks required to get to the event. Guided the teams to keep them on track with good communication, teaching, writing, communication, and data collection skills.

Add your accomplishments at the end of each job block.

WHAT TO INCLUDE IN YOUR FEDERAL RESUME

Work Experience: Federal jobs often require that you have experience in a particular type of work for a certain period of time. You must show how your skills and experiences **meet the qualifications and requirements listed in the job announcement** to be considered for the job.

Include dates, hours, level of experience, and examples for each work experience. For each work experience you list, make sure you include:

- Start and end dates (including the month and year)
- The number of hours you worked per week
- The level and amount of experience–for instance, whether you served as a project manager or a team member helps to illustrate your level of experience
- Examples of relevant experiences and accomplishments that prove you can perform the tasks at the level required for the job as stated in the job announcement. Your experience needs to address every required qualification

Example

Program Analyst GS-343-11
Name of organization and office, street address, city, state, zip
January 2009 – Present 40 Hours/Week
$63,000/Year (optional)
Experience/Accomplishment

Include volunteer work and roles in community organizations

Don't limit yourself to only including paid work experience. Include relevant volunteer work or community organization roles that demonstrate your ability to do the job.

Education

College or University, city, state, zip code

- Title of degree or certification, month, and year
- Type of degree or certification, total credits earned
- Major Courses; descriptions of Capstone or major course projects
- Copy of your transcript should be uploaded into USAJOBS.

Other Qualifications

- Job-related training courses (title and year/classroom hours and certificate)
- Job-related skills: languages, computer skills, typing speed, technical skills
- Job-related certifications and licenses
- Job-related honors, awards, and special accomplishments
- Job-related volunteer or activities. Leadership activities, public speaking, performance awards (give dates, but do not send documents unless requested).

JULIA ANN MARIE KELLY
FEDERAL RESUME CASE STUDY #3

Hiring Authority: Native American, 30% or More Disabled Veteran

Current Position: Ammunitions Test Coordinator

Current Non-Profit Volunteer Position: Current Non-Profit Volunteer Position: Vice President, Native American Women Warriors

Target: Veteran's Administration, Senior Program Analyst, Center for Women Veterans, GS-14

Kathryn Troutman, Federal Career Coach®, reviewed Julia's job announcement and her current resume which focused on 10 years of Ammunition Test Coordination work for the military and then as a contractor. At the bottom of the resume, there was a short list of non-profit organizations and events with some dates. No duties or challenges for the non-profits. The announcement that Julia sent was for a GS-14, Women's Veteran Center, Senior Program Analyst. A coach at the VA was helping Julia with her Federal resume giving her minor points about keywords in the Ammunition sections of the resume. This was NOT going to get her Best Qualified. With my direction, Julia begin to build out the non-profit sections of the resume into real "job blocks" with job duties, accomplishments, hours per week, and dates. The non-profit positions were listed first on the resume above her prior work in Ammunition Testing so that the HR reviewers could see her solid and expert experience in Veteran Women's Non-Profits and Native American Veteran Women's Non-Profits. This was an Extreme Career Change job application because her current position was Ammunition Test Coordinator for the US Army Redstone Test Center.

TARGET POSITION DESCRIPTION

The resume has to match the position description qualifications, plus the knowledge, skills and abilities.

15. Classified/Graded by	Official Title of Position	Pay Plan	Occupational Code	Grade	Initials	Date
a. Office of Personnel Management						
b. Department, Agency or Establishment	Program Analyst	GS	0343	14	DAM	08/30/2018
c. Second Level Review						
d. First Level Review						
e. Recommended by Supervisor or Initiating Office	Program Analyst	GS	0343	14		

16. Organizational Title of Position *(if different from official title)*	17. Name of Employee *(if vacant, specify)*
Senior Program Analyst	

18. Department, Agency, or Establishment	c. Third Subdivision
Department of Veterans Affairs	
a. First Subdivision	**d. Fourth Subdivision**
Office of the Secretary	
b. Second Subdivision	**e. Fifth Subdivision**
Center for Women Veterans	

Position Description

Senior Program Analyst, GS-343-14

Department of Veterans Affairs
Office of the Secretary
Center for Women Veterans

<u>Introduction:</u>

This position is located in the Center for Women Veterans, in Washington, DC. The Center's responsibilities are to assess women Veterans' services within and outside the Department on an ongoing basis, and to assure that VA policy and planning practices address the needs of women. The incumbent serves as a Program Analyst to the Director, Center for Women Veterans and provides the Center's Director and Associate Director with support, assistance, and advice in a variety of operational and management areas. The incumbent is also responsible for developing, analyzing, monitoring, and tracking the Center's performance.

Principal Duties and Responsibilities

Program Planning, Analysis and Development (60%)

Performs analyses of ongoing Center operations and develops reports: (1) regarding Center programs towards accomplishing goals and; (2) making recommendations for broad changes in goals and/or approaches towards achieving the goals. Participates in developing long and short-range plans, and performance goals and objectives of the Center for Women Veterans. Develops, implement, and provides ongoing evaluation of specific programs and services designed to improve agency performance of the Center for Women Veterans. Participates with the Director and Associate Director in formulating and recommending policy and procedures that will promote the development of the most effective and efficient programs possible for the Center. Provides technical guidance on plans, policies, and procedures related to Center activities. Designs systems to track and evaluate the success of women's initiatives and inquiries.

Program Communication (30%)
Reviews and independently develops all types of executive level correspondence reports, briefings, proposal packages, and other communications. Gathers background material on a wide range of subjects for the Director to present to the Department and professional groups. Coordinates, consolidates and reviews documents for the approval of both the Director and Associate Director, Center for Women Veterans.

Provides efficient, timely, and cost-effective general administrative support services. Serves as a resource expert in all areas of the Center.

- Prepares analytical, technical, and administrative duties in the budget administration process including budget formulation, justification, presentation, and execution for the Center.

- Administers and monitors education and training programs for Center employees.

- Reviews all actions managed by the Director of the Center for Women Veterans to ensure appropriate and accurate coordination.

Special Projects (10%)

Serve as a project leader on various projects with responsibility for directing and monitoring the development and accomplishment of employee training related to the project. Monitor projects status and adjust work plans for project accomplishment. Review all projects managed by the Director and the Associate Director to ensure appropriate and accurate coordination.

Factor 1-8 Knowledge Required by the Position

(1) Mastery of a wide range of qualitative and/or quantitative methods for the assessment and improvement of program effectiveness or the improvement of complex management processes and systems; (2) Comprehensive knowledge of the range of administration laws, policies, regulations, and precedents applicable to the administration of VA program; (3) Knowledge of Center's program goals and objectives, the sequence and timing of key program events and milestones, and methods of evaluating the worth of program accomplishments; and (4) Skill to plan, organize, and direct team study work and to negotiate effectively with management to accept and implement recommendations where the proposals involve substantial agency resources, require extensive changes in established procedures, or may be in conflict with the desires of the activity studied.

BEFORE AND AFTER KEYWORDS

BEFORE RESUME KEYWORDS

- AMMUNITION TEST COORDINATOR
- ENGINEERING, RESEARCH & CONSULTING (ERC) INC.
- PROGRAM PLANNING
- PROGRAM ANALYSIS
- DEVELOPMENT
- PROGRAM COMMUNICATION
- JOINT TEST TEAM
- SPECIAL PROJECTS: Created database of excess ammunition stored at Redstone Arsenal Test Center. Update data base monthly to create reports for US Army Test and Evaluation Command. Research and analyze data for recommendations to remove ammunition from inventory. I was instrumental in a Lean Six Sigma second evaluation of an Ammunition Process Improvement with a certified Quality Engineer.

AFTER KEYWORDS - *TARGETED*

- DEVELOP GOALS
- SENIOR ADVISOR
- DESIGNED OPERATIONAL PLANS
- EVALUATE PERFORMANCE
- DESIGN SYSTEMS AND DATA TO EVALUATE PROGRAMS
- FORMULATE POLICIES TO IMPROVE WOMEN'S INITIATIVES
- DIRECT ADMINISTRATIVE OPERATIONS
- WRITE AND EDIT MEMORANDA AND REPORTS
- DIRECT SPECIAL PROJECTS

BEFORE AND AFTER ORGANIZATION

BEFORE RESUME ORGANIZATION

- OBJECTIVE
- EDUCATION
- TRAINING
- GOVERNMENT CONTRACTING EXPERIENCE
- MILITARY EXPERIENCE
- PROFESSIONAL MEMBERSHIPS
- CONFERENCES
- PRESENTATIONS
- INTERNATIONAL TRAVEL
- SPECIAL INTERESTS
- VOLUNTEER SERVICES
- CRITICAL SKILLS

AFTER RESUME ORGANIZATION

- OBJECTIVE
- CRITICAL SKILLS
- SPECIAL INTERESTS
- PROFESSIONAL MEMBERSHIPS
- CONFERENCES
- PRESENTATIONS
- INTERNATIONAL TRAVEL
- NATIVE AMERICAN VETERANS SERVICES / PROGRAM MANAGEMENT
- AMMUNITION TEST COORDINATOR, CONTRACTOR

BEFORE RESUME

Julia was an Ammunition Test Coordinator and VERY active Volunteer for First Nation Women Warriors. Here is a Partial BEFORE Resume.

EMPLOYMENT EXPERIENCE
AMMUNITION TEST COORDINATOR, Contractor
Engineering, Research & Consulting (ERC) Inc.
U.S. Army Redstone Test Center, Joint Test Management Office, Redstone Arsenal, AL
07/2018 to Present, 40 hours per week, $75,088
Supervisor: Kevin Tate, 555-666-8888, Permission to contact

PROGRAM PLANNING: Begin project planning when request for test services is submitted by the customer. Coordinate with account managers and directorate test coordinators to ensure customer requirements with cost estimate, test plans, and requisition for ammunition items are completed. Use regulations, procedures and methodologies regarding system test and evaluation regulations and test plans, safety, security, storage, inventory management, shipments, handling, issuing, and receiving ammunition.

BEFORE RESUME CONT.

PROGRAM ANALYSIS: Performed analysis on the ammunition management in test project programs. Developed and implemented work procedures for test coordinator position. Developed and implemented management and project close out training to directorate test coordinators. Provide ongoing evaluation of the process of ammunition management in the Test Program Integration Directorate. Provide technical guidance with test plans, procedures and policies. I am considered the SUBJECT MATTER EXPERT regarding ammunition management.

DEVELOPMENT: Developed, wrote, and implemented work procedures for ammunition test coordinator position. The result is a first time documented process regarding ammunition management in the five phases of test management. Developed logistical plans and identified the cause of delay in testing and the impact of the delays to support the test efforts. Developed long term cost proposals to customers for storage, inventory, and maintenance of ammunition beyond scheduled testing dates. Developed, integrated, and implemented solutions to diverse, highly complex problems across multiple areas and disciplines. Developed and implemented new techniques to fit new situations to improve ammunition management in the test life cycle. Developed ammunition management training plan at the Test Coordinator level. This training was implemented at mass training sessions.

I received four monetary incentive pay awards and two pay raises for these accomplishments from my contracting company.

SPECIAL PROJECTS: Create database of excess ammunition stored at Redstone Arsenal Test Center. Update database monthly to create reports for U.S. Army Test and Evaluation Command. Research and analyze data for recommendations to remove ammunition from inventory. I was instrumental in a Lean Six Sigma second evaluation of an Ammunition Process Improvement with a Quality Engineer certified in Quality processes.

PROFESSIONAL MEMBERSHIPS
Disabled American Veterans, Women Veterans Interactive, Veterans of Foreign Wars, Society of the first Infantry Division, US Army Ordnance Corps Regimental Society, Trickster Cultural Center.

CONFERENCES
Tribal Veterans Benefit training, Montana, VA; 3rd Annual Women Veterans Health Mini Expo; Understanding the Role of Social Support in Veterans' Well-Being: The Development and Implementation of the Women Veterans Network; Domestic Violence and Disabilities; FB Women Veteran Series: Resources for Appeals, Mental Health, MST & Supporting Spouses; FB Veteran Series: Resources for Homeless and At-Risk Veterans; FB Women Veteran Series: Women's Reproductive & Whole Health Resources; 6th Annual National Gathering of Native Veterans.

PRESENTATIONS
Missing Murdered Indigenous Women Presentation to American Association University Women; Domestic Violence Exhibit Opening in Schaumburg, IL

INTERNATIONAL TRAVEL
75th Anniversary of D-Day with a Native Veteran Delegation

SPECIAL INTERESTS
Advocate for Veterans. I counsel veterans in need of resources. I am active in Native American traditions. I travel to color guard, guest speak, and perform dance for events. I work with the Trickster Cultural Center in Schaumburg, IL regarding different grant requirements and Native American Veteran issues with concentration in women veteran issues.

VOLUNTEER SERVICES
11/2010 to 4/2014 Vice President of Native American Women Warriors non-profit organization. I developed the organization plan and submitted the plan for non-profit designation. I did this work full-time while caring for an ailing parent.

1/2011 to 12/2011 Adjutant for Chapter 10 Disabled American Veterans.

5/2014 to 9/2016 Secretary and Treasurer for First Nations Women Warriors. I developed the organization plan and submitted for non-profit designation. I did this work full-time until I moved to get a government contract job 4/2016.

AFTER RESUME

Julia's after resume required a total reorganization. The new resume is targeted. It lists her critical skills, including software knowledge, first. Below is a partial AFTER resume.

JULIA
street address
City, State, zip
Home Telephone
email
30% or More Disabled Veteran

OBJECTIVE: Senior Program Analyst, Veterans Administration, GS-343-14

CRITICAL SKILLS

Project Management	Budget Analysis	Microsoft Excel
Research and Analysis	Drafting Cost Estimates	Problem Solving
Data Mining	Public Speaking	Teamwork
Critical Thinking	Emotional Intelligence	Writing

SPECIAL INTERESTS
Volunteer work/community involvement; Traveling, Native American ceremonies and events.

PROFESSIONAL MEMBERSHIPS
Disabled American Veterans, Women Veterans Interactive, Veterans of Foreign Wars, Society of the First Infantry Division, and US Army Ordnance Corps Regimental Society.

CONFERENCES
Tribal Veterans Benefit training, Montana, VA; Virtual 3rd Annual Women Veterans Health Mini Expo, Birmingham, AL; Understanding the Role of Social Support in Veterans' Well-Being: The Development and Implementation of the Women Veterans Network; Domestic Violence and Disabilities; Facebook Veterans Affairs Women Veteran Series: Resources for Appeals, Mental Health, MST & Supporting Spouses, and Women's Reproductive & Whole Health Resources; Facebook Veteran Affairs Veteran Series: Resources for Homeless and At-Risk Veterans; Virtual 6th Annual National Gathering of Native Veterans.

PRESENTATIONS
Missing Murdered Indigenous Women Presentation to American Association University Women; Domestic Violence Exhibit Opening Trickster Cultural Center, Schaumburg, IL

INTERNATIONAL TRAVEL
75th Anniversary of D-Day Native Veteran Delegation supporting grant program "They Talk to Each Other."

NATIVE AMERICAN VETERANS SERVICES / PROGRAM MANAGEMENT

Vice President, Native American Women Warriors 11/2010 to 4/2014
P.O. Box 8145 Pueblo, CO 81008
Supervisor: Enola Jones, 777-555-8888, no contact
Hours per week: 40

Mission: A 501(c)(3) Non-Profit Organization to assist Native American women veterans in receiving help and tools to empower themselves; to take on modern challenges in education and employment; and to guide those needing special services.

DEVELOP GOALS: Developed the organization by-laws to submit for non-profit designation. Developed partnership with veteran and community organizations, businesses, Tribes, federal and local governments to provide project consultation, social, economic, and health training.

SENIOR ADVISOR: Provide advice on organizational mission and goals. Recommended strategic planning conference to establish the organization systems and processes.

DESIGNED OPERATIONAL PLANS: Attended strategic planning conference hosted by Native Strategies. Developed an organization operation plan to stand up Native American Women Warriors. The plan assisted the leadership team to organize, create, develop and implement processes, standard operating procedures, and create database to partner with other organizations.

EVALUATE PERFORMANCE: Analyze and review processes and standard operating procedures to ensure the organization is staying on track with mission and goals.

DESIGN SYSTEMS AND DATA TO EVALUATE PROGRAMS: Created after action reports, interviews, and surveys after every event to measure the effectiveness of the event and to determine if the organization is being run as intended and reaching its intended audience.

FORMULATE POLICIES TO IMPROVE WOMEN'S INITIATIVES: Native American Women Warriors members were invited to meet with congressional leaders in Washington DC. This visit resulted in creation of a women's mentorship program for the military members on active duty. Members met with the Veterans Affairs Office of Tribal Governmental Affairs to get briefed on current status of issues regarding Tribal veterans' access to Veterans Affairs Healthcare and benefits. An after action report was written and submitted to congressional leaders for action.

DIRECT ADMINISTRATIVE OPERATIONS: Assigned events and projects to members to coordinate and create agendas for the assigned event or project. Monitored their progress and advised when necessary.

WRITE AND EDIT MEMORANDUMS AND REPORTS: Wrote 24 after action reports upon completing events or projects. These reports were formulated from members input. Created and completed financial reports. Reviewed and edited standard operating procedures and agreements for the organization president.

DIRECT SPECIAL PROJECTS: Attended the NYC Veterans Day parade in 2010, and 2011. Attended the 2012 San Diego Veterans Day Parade. Attended the 2013 Inaugural Parade. These projects were a major undertaking by the organization with so many tasks required to get to the event. Members were given different tasks to pull together the whole project. I kept the team on track with good communication, teaching writing, communication, and data collection skills.

RESULTS

Success! Selected!

On Mon, Mar 1, 2021 at 2:14 PM, Julia wrote:

Hello Kathryn,

I want to thank you so much in getting this resume structured so I could have a chance at a GS14 Senior Program Analyst, Center of Women Veterans, Secretary of Veterans Affairs.

I was interviewed 11 Feb. The most difficult interview I have ever done. The first question: create a high level management tool to track 6-10 initiatives in the Center. You have 20 minutes. Yep. Whew!

I got called Thursday, 25Feb2021.
I was selected for the job.
I am like "Wow."
I would not have been able to do this without your help.

Thank you again. Julia

JUSTUS MARTIN
FEDERAL RESUME CASE STUDY #4

Hiring Authority: US Navy 30% or More Disabled and Military Spouse of Active Duty Military

Current Position: Census Enumerator, Home School Teacher

Target: National Park Service, Visual Information Specialist, GS-7

Mary Ann Bowersock, Veterans Employment Representative, Virginia Employment Commission, coached Justus for his Federal job search. At the time, she said, "Justus is looking for a Federal job. He is both a former Sailor and currently a military officer spouse (his wife is a Navy nurse). He is a Special Disabled Veteran (100 percent service connected but is able to work) and is my client via the VA's Veteran Readiness and Education Program that was formerly called Vocational Rehabilitation and Education."

QUALIFICATIONS REQUIRED

Education: Undergraduate and Graduate Education. Major study—commercial art, fine arts, art history, industrial design, architecture, drafting, interior design, photography, visual communication, or other fields related to the position.

GS-07
Specialized Experience: Applicants must have at least one year (52 weeks) of specialized experience at the next lower grade GS-05, or equivalent in other pay systems. Examples of specialized experience includes knowledge of basic principles, concepts, and practices of visual information, applying basic principles, concept and practices of the occupation sufficient to perform entry-level assignments in the production of visual products, a variety of art media, visual and audio aspects of publications, as well as exhibits or presentations.

BEFORE AND AFTER KEYWORDS

BEFORE RESUME KEYWORDS

- COMMUNICATIONS
- CENSUS ENUMERATOR
- INDEPENDENCE
- DIVERSITY
- POLICY ADHERENCE
- SEASONAL BOOKSELLER
- HOSPITAL CORPSMAN

AFTER KEYWORDS - *TARGETED*

- FILM AND VIDEO PRODUCTION
- LANDSCAPE AND PORTRAIT PHOTOGRAPHY
- AUDIO VISUAL DESIGN
- SOUND DESIGN AND ENGINEERING
- ADVANCED DIGITAL VIDEO PRODUCTION
- WRITER-EDITOR
- VIDEO PRODUCTION

BEFORE AND AFTER ORGANIZATION

BEFORE RESUME ORGANIZATION

- SKILLS, LEADERSHIP COMPETENCIES, AWARDS/ACHIEVEMENTS
- PROFESSIONAL EXPERIENCE
- VOLUNTEER EXPERIENCE
- ADDITIONAL EXPERIENCE
- EDUCATION

AFTER RESUME ORGANIZATION

- SKILLS, LEADERSHIP COMPETENCIES, AWARDS/ACHIEVEMENTS
- PROFESSIONAL EXPERIENCE
- VOLUNTEER EXPERIENCE
- ADDITIONAL EXPERIENCE
- EDUCATION

BEFORE RESUME

This resume is not targeted toward Visual Information Specialist (Digital). This is a reverse chronological listing of employment, with education at the end, and no technical equipment and skills featured. This is a typical "down the middle" resume that is not targeted toward any particular position.

Justus Martin

Address, city, state, zip 123-456-7890 name@name.com

Communications

■ ■ ■ **Finding the Right People... Using the Best Channels... Delivering Results** ■ ■ ■

Natural leader, innovator, communicator, and relationship builder ... OSHA 10 Certified... USN Veteran

SKILLS	LEADERSHIP COMPETENCIES	AWARDS/ ACHIEVEMENTS
Communication	Supervising Others	Navy Letter of Commendation for participation on Vaccination Team
Microsoft Office	Conflict Resolution	Navy Good Conduct
Data Collection	Emotional Intelligence	
Writing	Communication Skills	
Reading Comprehension	Manage Performance	
Critical Thinking	Interviewing Skills	
Oral Comprehension	Team Building	
	Delegation	

Professional Experience

CENSUS ENUMERATOR (09/2020 to 10/2020), **United States Census Bureau,** Stafford, VA. Hours/Week: 40+. Salary: 25/hr.
Position Scope: Followed Federal guidelines to ensure that the centennial census was carried out and completed in a timely manner. Worked with very little supervision while conducting interviews among diverse populations. Safe-guarded private information in accordance with federal guidelines while ensuring government property was protected and accounted for.

- INDEPENDENCE: Received work for the day and made plans to carry out workload in the most effective manner. This included planning routes, organizing workload by proximity and planning for unforeseen circumstances. Minimal oversight was required, and independent working was preferred. Contacted individuals to be interviewed at home by telephone or in person; assisted individuals in completing questionnaires. Reviewed data obtained from interview for completeness and accuracy. Collected and analyzed data, tallying the number of citizens for census. Located and listed addresses and households. Identified and reported problems and resolved inconsistencies in interviewees' responses. Completed an average of 25 cases a day, 125 a week.
- DIVERSITY: Interviewed a diverse population of people including different religions, sexes, orientations and races. Built and maintained rapport with different communities throughout the state of Virginia. Utilized a variety of interpersonal skills to connect to census respondent. Asked questions in accordance with instructions to obtain various specified information, such as person's name, address, age, religious preference, or state of residency.
- POLICY ADHERENCE: Followed all guidelines in accordance with federal regulations to best protect personal and sensitive information obtained through interviews. Took steps to safeguard government property from theft or sabotage. Identified and reported problems and resolved inconsistencies in interviewees' responses. Compiled, recorded, and coded results or data from interview using computer or specified forms.

SEASONAL BOOKSELLER (10/2018 to 2/2019), **Barnes and Nobles,** Otay Ranch, CA. Hours/Week: 25. Salary: 12.00/hr.
Position Scope: Provided excellent customer service as a bookseller, supporting management team in day to day operations. Maintained hygiene, security and coverage of assigned daily sections. Warmly greeted and assisted customers, ensuring all needs were met. Made recommendations to customers based on product preferences. Constructed book, magazine and holiday displays according to organizational policies.

- COMMUNICATION: Designed and conducted special children's activities such as storytelling hours, book talks and puppet show. Tailored each event toward a broad range of audience members including parents, children and children with special needs. Took steps to evaluate, format and organize content to fit audience ages and understanding. Used nonconfrontational deescalating techniques for unruly audience members.

- INITIATIVE: Created a monthly game night which boosted customer retention, attendance, and spending at the onsite café.
- DEPENDABILITY: Demonstrated a pattern of goal completion that led to being tasked with more senior tasks such as building displays, taking point on ordering supplies and manning the customer service line. This freed up many associates to focus more on customer satisfaction, membership sales and store hygiene, all which improved exponentially.

HOSPITAL CORPSMAN/DENTIAL TECHICIAN (11/2009 to 11/2013), *United States Navy*, Bethesda, MD Hours/Week: 25. Salary: 24,512 USD Per Year

Position Scope: Performed a diverse group of duties and jobs while serving as a corpsman. Succeeded in interpreting and executing all the basic functions of a dental corpsman as well as a ward corpsman. Functions included basic oral hygiene care, chairside assisting, and sterilization techniques. Ward corpsman duties included running a 15-bed unit, ensuring patient care accuracy and basic supply management. Other areas of duties included records management and front desk management.

- LEADERSHIP: Managed team of three to four junior sailors in completion of their duties. Ensured training was up to date and encouraged exploration of different fields and interests. Team members consistently scored high on advancement exams and regularly received high promotional recommendations.
- ORGANIZATION: Succeeded in constructing and maintaining as many as 8,000 medical and dental records. Helped to expend the electronic records system at Walter Reed National Military Medical Center, easing the overall burden on records technicians and helping with loss prevention.

Volunteer Experience

CONTRIBUTING WRITER

Position Scope: Worked as a junior writer as part of volunteer on the job training. Sought out material for publication, interviewed potential story sources, and worked to construct print and digital distribution copies.

INTEGRITY: Maintained professional journalistic integrity when preparing a story or feature by ensuring that all consideration was paid to accuracy, currency, authority, and coverage. Adhering to these guidelines helped to ensure that the message was disseminated with as much factual integrity as possible.

EVALUATE CONTENT, FORMAT, AND ORGANIZATIONAL PUBLICATIONS: Reviewed publications to determine the content matched the source for accuracy and met all standards of publication. Arranged written articles to adhere to format proposed by current guidelines and took swift action to correct any formatting issues in a timely manner. Established identifiable goals to ensure that written articles were organized in a manner conducive to readability and understanding.

CRITICAL ANALYSIS: Analyzed final products after production and identified elements of content, format, organization and presentation that needed improvement. Observed 3 cases in which a junior sailor misattributed quote. Analyzing the final product ensured the integrity of the paper remained intact.

Additional Experience

- Assisted 15+ disabled veterans in filing disability and compensation claims or appealing unfavorable claims decisions.
- Mentored several veterans on the processes and procedures for acquiring Vocational Rehabilitation and Employment through the Veteran's Affairs Agency.
- Wrote and directed short film "The Unbowed" shown at the *Guam International Film Festival.*
- Directed and edited script for "Scared to Death" shown at the *Guam International Film Festival.*

Education

Certificate of Completion - *Film and Video* - **Full Sail University**, *July 2020 - GPA, 3.93*
Bachelor of Science - *Media Arts in Digital Video Production* - **Platt College San Diego**, *April 2020 - GPA, 3.88*
Bachelor of Arts - *Mass Communication* - **University of Maryland University College**, *May 2018 - GPA, 3.0*
Associates of Arts - *General Studies* - **Central Texas College**, *May 2015 - GPA, 3.20*

AFTER RESUME

Justus's AFTER resume is targeted, with his equipment skills first, followed by his education and academic projects. All of this comes before his work experience.

JUSTUS MARTIN

Address Line 1 • Address Line 2

123-456-7890 • name@name.com

30% or More Disabled • EO 13473 Eligible, Military Spouse

PROFILE

Communicator • Writer • Editor • Audiovisual Storyteller

SOFTWARE AND EQUIPMENT LIST

EQUIPMENT
Sony FS5
Manfrotto tripod (standard and electric)
Box lights and fill light (3-point lighting setup)
Green and blue screen sheets with steel frames
Lavalier microphone
Shotgun microphone
Boom microphone and attachments
Steady shot (rig and harness)

SOFTWARE
Adobe - Photoshop
- Premier
- After Effects
- Media Encoder

Microsoft - Word, Excel, PowerPoint
Sound Editing: Pro Tools
Script Writing: Final Draft
Film Pre-Production Software
- Magic Scheduling
- Magic Budget

3D Design: Maya

EDUCATION

CERTIFICATE, *Film and Video Production* • July 2020
Full Sail University • Winter Park, FL • GPA: 3.93

- Relevant Coursework: History of Motion Picture Arts, Introduction to Film and Video, Scriptwriting Techniques, New Media Tools, Introduction to Post-production, Project I: Film and Video, Portfolio I: Film and Video.

BACHELOR OF SCIENCE, *Media Arts in Digital Video Production* • April 2020
Platt College • San Diego, CA • GPA: 3.88

- Relevant Coursework: Reporting & Writing the News, Documentary Process, Broadcast Journalism, Media Computer Graphics, Broadcast Production, Advertising in Mass Media, Interpersonal Communication, Mass Media Law.

ACADEMIC PROJECTS

LANDSCAPE AND PORTRAIT PHOTOGRAPHY: Utilized scouting techniques to determine best location to photograph subjects. Ensured every effort was taken to meet the criteria for project assignment. Used safety checklist to ensure shoot was within safety standards. Conducted research to determine the legality of location photography and filed correct forms when appropriate.

AUDIO VISUAL DESIGN: Created mini documentary on the operating procedures of street canvassers working with the Save the Children organization. Conducted numerous meetings with office managers and directors reviewing project logistics. Ensured correct legal paperwork was filed, such as release forms and Hold Harmless agreements. Used Creative Cloud to edit picture and sound.

SOUND DESIGN AND ENGINEERING: Final project for sound design and engineering. Reviewed movie clips and selected and documented sounds to be replaced. Utilized state of the art recording booth and Pro tools program to recreate and edit sounds. Created Foley sound effects. Procured sounds from third party taking care to consider copyright laws. Categorized sound effects to ensure organization and proper workflow. Used Adobe programs to adjust pitch, volume, gain and clarity.

ADVANCED DIGITAL VIDEO PRODUCTION: Capstone Project that consisted of a month-long short film production. Wrote and edited script using a word processing program. Created a casting call and auditioned actors and actresses according to audition edict. Scouted location, contacted owner and filed correct paperwork. Created custom costumes and ensured actor and actress comfortability. Commissioned custom set design to enhance production design of the short film.

EXPERIENCE

CENSUS ENUMERATOR — **09/2020 – 12/2020**
U.S. Census Bureau • Stafford, VA — 40 Hours per Week
Supervisor: Bob Boberson (321-321-3213) — $25 per Hour

Followed Federal guidelines to ensure that the centennial census was carried out and completed in a timely manner. Worked with very little supervision while conducting interviews among diverse populations. Safe-guarded private information in accordance with federal guidelines while ensuring the protection and accountability of government property.

PLANNING & LOGISTICS: Received work for the day and made plans to carry out workload in the most effective manner. This included planning routes, organizing workload by proximity and planning for unforeseen circumstances. Minimal oversight was required, and independent working was preferred. Contacted individuals to be interviewed at home by telephone or in-person; assisted individuals in completing questionnaires.

DATA REVIEW & ANALYSIS: Reviewed data obtained from interview for completeness and accuracy. Collected and analyzed data, tallying the number of citizens for decennial (10 year) census. Located and listed addresses and-households. Identified and reported problems and resolved inconsistencies.

INTERPERSONAL COMMUNICATION: Interviewed a diverse population of people including different religions, sexes, orientations and races. Built and maintained rapport with different communities throughout the state of Virginia. Utilized a variety of interpersonal skills to connect to census respondent. Asked questions in accordance with instructions to obtain various specified information, such as person's name, address, age, religious preference, or state of residency.

REGULATORY & LEGAL COMPLIANCE: Followed all guidelines in accordance with federal regulations to best protect personal and sensitive information obtained through interviews. Presented limited and repetitive pre-established talking points to explain the purpose of the census to respondent. Took steps to safeguard government property from theft or sabotage. Compiled, recorded, and coded results or data from interview using computer or specified forms.

DENTAL TECHNICIAN — **11/2009 – 11/2013**
U.S. Navy • Bethesda, MD — 25 Hours per Week
Supervisor: Mike Mikerson (098-765-4321) — $25,000 per Year

Performed a diverse group of duties and jobs while serving as a corpsman. Succeeded in interpreting and executing all the basic functions of a dental and ward corpsman. Functions included basic oral hygiene care, chair-side assisting and sterilization techniques. Other duties included records management and front desk management.

SUPERVISION & TRAINING: Supervised a team of 3-4 junior sailors in completion of their duties. Ensured training and competencies were up to date. Organized physical training sessions and counseling based off of needs. Team members consistently scored high on advancement exams and regularly received high promotional recommendations.

RECORDS MANAGEMENT & OVERSIGHT: Succeeded in constructing and maintaining as many as 8,000 medical and dental records. Helped to expend the electronic records system at Walter Reed National Military Medical Center, helping with loss prevention. Examined and expanded records room policies on filing and organizing. Conducted research on best practices being utilized at other commands and helped advise proponents on the preparation and distribution of published policies.

ADDITIONAL HIGHLIGHTS

- Received writer credits for work titled "The Good Son" published in *Storyboard: A Journal of Pacific Imagery.*
- Received writer credits for work entitled "Fire and Brimstone" Published in *Gryphon's Magazine.*
- Wrote and directed short film "The Unbowed" shown at the *Guam International Film Festival.*
- Directed and edited script for "Scared to Death" shown at the *Guam International Film Festival.*
- Assisted 15+ disabled veterans in filing disability and compensation claims or appealing unfavorable claims decisions.
- Coached 30+ disabled veterans on applying for the vocation and rehabilitation program.

RESULTS

Justus's 6-month National Park Service (NPS) position has now turned into a 10-month temporary position with NPS. He can apply for a GS-9 position after one year.

SAMPLE OUTLINE FORMAT FEDERAL RESUME

TARGET: US Army E-6 - Seeking First Federal Career as Aviation Safety Inspector (General Aviation Maintenance), FG-9

JOSEPH ROBERTSON
1234 Spruce Street
Turtlelake, NJ 08640
Home Phone: (111) 111-1234 | Work Phone: (111) 111-2345 | jrobertson@gmail.com

QUALIFICATIONS SUMMARY

Avionics Test Station and Component Craftsman / Electronic Integrated System Mechanic with 20+ years of experience inspecting, testing, troubleshooting, repairing, modifying, and maintaining complex integrated electronic aviation systems for the U.S. Air Force (USAF). Experienced in lifecycle maintenance planning, scheduling, and management of sophisticated electronic systems. Advanced analytical, troubleshooting, and problem-solving skills. Ability to instruct and supervise less experienced technicians.

- Track record of performing the most difficult and complex Electronic Integrated System Mechanic tasks and producing superior results in a fast-paced, quality-driven environment. Excellent safety record.
- Advanced technical skills in the use of computer-controlled diagnostic automated test equipment (ATE) and a wide variety of hand and power tools.
- Completed numerous aviation systems technical certifications, including 7-Level Communication and Navigation Systems Craftsman. AAS degree, Avionics Systems Technology expected in 7/2021.
- Hands-on experience with the following aircraft and related systems: A-10 Thunderbolt II, B-1B Lancer, B-2 Spirit, C-130 Hercules, C-17 Globemaster III, CV-22 Osprey, and F-16 C/D Viper.

TECHNICAL CERTIFICATIONS

Communication and Navigation Systems Craftsman, 7-Level Certification, 2007 | C-130 Self-Contained Navigation Systems Certified, 2007 | AN/APN 59 Radar System Certified, 2007 | Basic Soldering Technique Certified, 2007 | AN/ARC-164 UHF Radio Certified, 2007 | F-16 Improved Avionics Intermediate Station Certified, 2007 | Air Force Smart Operations (AFOC) 21, Green Belt Certification, 2014 | Block II/III Supply Certification, 2018.

PROFESSIONAL EXPERIENCE

C-17 AVIONICS TEST STATION AND COMPONENT CRAFTSMAN (2A071K) — 02/2018 to Present
U.S. Air Force (USAF), 305th Maintenance Squadron, Avionics Maintenance Flight — Annual Salary: $46,000
Joint Base McGuire-Dix-Lakehurst (JB MDL), Trenton, NJ — 40 hours per week
Supervisor: Bob Thompson, 111-222-3456; Permission to contact

AIRCRAFT MAINTENANCE – MILITARY REPAIR STATION – TEAM SUPERVISION: Supervise 6-member team of technicians comprised of Active Duty, Reserve, and civilian personnel in the maintenance, alignment, calibration, troubleshooting, modification, and repair of avionics test systems, test stations, Special Equipment (SE), and aircraft components for 14 assigned and transient C-17 Globemaster III military transport aircraft. Plan, organize, and implement all integrated avionics activities, including the physical layout of facilities. Ensure SE and spare parts availability.

MAINTENANCE AND REPAIR OF AIRCRAFT SYSTEMS WITH RESPONSIBILITY FOR CERTIFYING AIRWORTHINESS: Perform operational tests on test equipment, SE, and aircraft components using a variety of test devices. Determine condition, evaluate performance, and isolate malfunctions in radar, sensors, communications, weapons control, electronic warfare (EW), flight control, and engine control systems. Analyze fault data received from test stations and document and troubleshoots procedures and determine most effective solution to effectively repair line replaceable units (LRUs).

AUTOMATED TEST EQUIPMENT (ATE): Use self-test and software functions, computer and manually operated avionics test equipment, SE, and test measurement and diagnostic equipment to determine scope of repair and required adjustments. Remove and replace assembly components using hand tools, soldering devices, and a variety of electronic instruments. Load computer programs.

TECHNICAL DOCUMENTS AND REPORTS: Initiate deficiency reports, maintenance analysis documents, technical data changes, and equipment records. Use the Reliability, Availability, Maintainability for Pods (RAMPOD) system to record relevant data. Prepare reports relating to environmental health and safety (EHS), security, Technical Orders, handling/use and disposal of hazardous waste and materials, and other applicable maintenance, training, procedures, standards, directives, and policies.

KEY ACCOMPLISHMENTS:

- Successfully aligned, calibrated, troubleshot, and repaired a C-17 automated test station valued at $9M, ensuring efficient operations.
- Led 4-person repair team that restored M967 maintenance test set capabilities, eliminating a 20-item critical asset backlog and a 3-day stand-still in maintenance production for a cost savings of $500K.
- Led regional Avionics flight daily maintenance operations. Efficiently repaired 60 units, saving $5M. Concurrently provide critical maintenance support for a multinational C-17 mobility exercise.
- Through effective training of 4-personnel, turned-in 367 Due-In-From Maintenance (DIFM) assets, enabling AF to reclaim $38M in depot-level cost.
- Led avionics maintenance support for 38 Hurricane Harvey relief missions, which ensured on-time delivery of 500 tons of airlifted cargo.

F-16 AVIONICS TEST STATION AND COMPONENT CRAFTSMAN (2A071K) 02/2017 to 02/2018
U.S. Air Force (USAF), 8th Maintenance Squadron, Avionics Maintenance Flight (AMF) Annual Salary: $46,000
Kunsan Air Base, Republic of South Korea 40 Hours per week
Supervisor: Mike Abramson (South Korea), 234-111-1111; Permission to contact

MAINTANANCE OVERSIGHT: Oversaw all activities for the maintenance, repair, overhaul, modification, inspection, testing, alignment, calibration, and troubleshooting of F-16 C/D aircraft and associated equipment. Oversaw receipt of parts through final inspection and sign-off for the intermediate-level repair of 1,100 specific aircraft avionics system line replaceable units (LRUs) in support of 44 assigned F-16C/D aircraft valued over $1.2B. Analyzed, inspected, tested, and troubleshot aircraft avionic system LRUs using handbooks, specifications, and technical orders (TOs) to formulate component operation.

CREW SUPERVISION: Provided accurate, effective technical and administrative direction to 10 subordinate maintenance technicians. Managed shift schedules, maintenance workloads, and training requirements. Established performance goals and evaluated performance. Ensured health, safety, and security procedures were in place and enforced. Performed quality control inspections to ensure compliance with Air Force standards, safety, and security protocols.

SUBJECT MATTER EXPERTISE: Managed all operations of two Improved Avionics Intermediate Test Stations (AIS) and associated support equipment worth $18M. Supervised all parts requisition and test station maintenance decisions. Tracked deficiency and catalogued data on aircraft grounded resulting from errors in units under the Squadron's maintenance authority. Oversaw quality, accuracy, currency of data, and regulatory and environmental compliance for the 21 programs.

KEY ACCOMPLISHMENTS:

- Led Upgrade of AIS: Led 3-member Time Compliance Technical Order (TCTO) systems software upgrade team that modified two test stations in 3 hours; 50% less time than the standard. Full capabilities were restored within a single shift.
- Directed accurate and efficient maintenance on 217 LRUs, filling 19 critical repair demands and saving$1.7M in supply costs. Achieved the best record in 7th Air Force.
- Oversaw maintenance of 426 LRUs in 2016. Repaired 55%; a 43% increase from 2015 for a cost savings of $4.2M in depot exchange costs.
- Developed innovative Excel spreadsheet that optimized Repair Network Integration metrics by demonstrating product trends, which reduced annual station operational costs and saved $56K.

F-16 AVIONICS TEST STATION AND COMPONENT CRAFTSMAN (2A071K) 09/2014 to 02/2017
USAF, Holloman Air Force Base, 54th Maintenance Squadron Annual Salary: $46,000 annually
Avionics Maintenance Flight, Alamogordo, NM 88310 40 hours per week

MANAGING FLIGHT CHIEF: Supervised and performed all activities for the repair, overhaul, rebuild, modification, testing, troubleshooting, removal, replacement, alignment, calibration, inspection of avionics integrated electronic and environmental systems, components, and subassemblies for 44 F-16C/D aircraft valued over $1.2B. Supervised an 8FW intermediate-level mx of 1.1K LRUs in support of assigned aircraft. Managed operations of two Improved Avionics Intermediate Shop (IAIS) Test Stations and associated support equipment worth $18M.

TEST STATION MAINTENANCE: Performed operational tests on test equipment, SE, and aircraft components using a variety of test devices. Determined condition, evaluated performance, and isolated malfunctions in radar, sensors, communications, weapons control, electronic warfare (EW), flight control, and engine control systems. Traced logic, schematics, test flow, and wiring diagrams. Documented and troubleshot procedures. Determined most effective solution to effectively repair LRUs. Performed test station maintenance.

ADDITIONAL INFORMATION

TECHNICAL SKILLS: Skilled in the interpretation of wiring and schematic diagrams, as well as utilizing and instructing others in the use of hand and power tools. I also have extensive experience with specialized test equipment such as O-scopes, pulse generators, power supplies, resistance decades, electrostatic field meters, digital/analog multimeters, precision measurement tools, and test equipment.

U.S. MILITARY SERVICE U.S. Air Force, 09/1998–Present; Retirement Date: 9/2021
Service includes two tours of duty to the Republic of South Korea, 2005 and 2017.

MILITARY HONORS AND AWARDS: Air Force (AF) Achievement Medal (2) | AF Outstanding Unit Award (6) | AF Good Conduct Medal (6) | National Defense Service Medal | Global War on Terrorism Service Medal | Korean Defense Service Medal | AF Overseas Ribbon Short | AF Longevity Service (4) | USAF NCO PME Graduate Ribbon | AF Training Ribbon

VOLUNTEER LEADERSHIP: Led volunteer team in renovating the local zoo's Aviary and Primate Exhibits, which saved $1.3K in 2017; Meal on Wheels Program Volunteer, Holloman AFB, 2015–2016; Intramural Bowling team captain, USAF, 2017-2018; Team Member, "Pats Run." Raised $1.3M for the Pat Tillman Military Scholarship Fund, 2015.

JONATHAN CRAFT
FEDERAL RESUME CASE STUDY #6

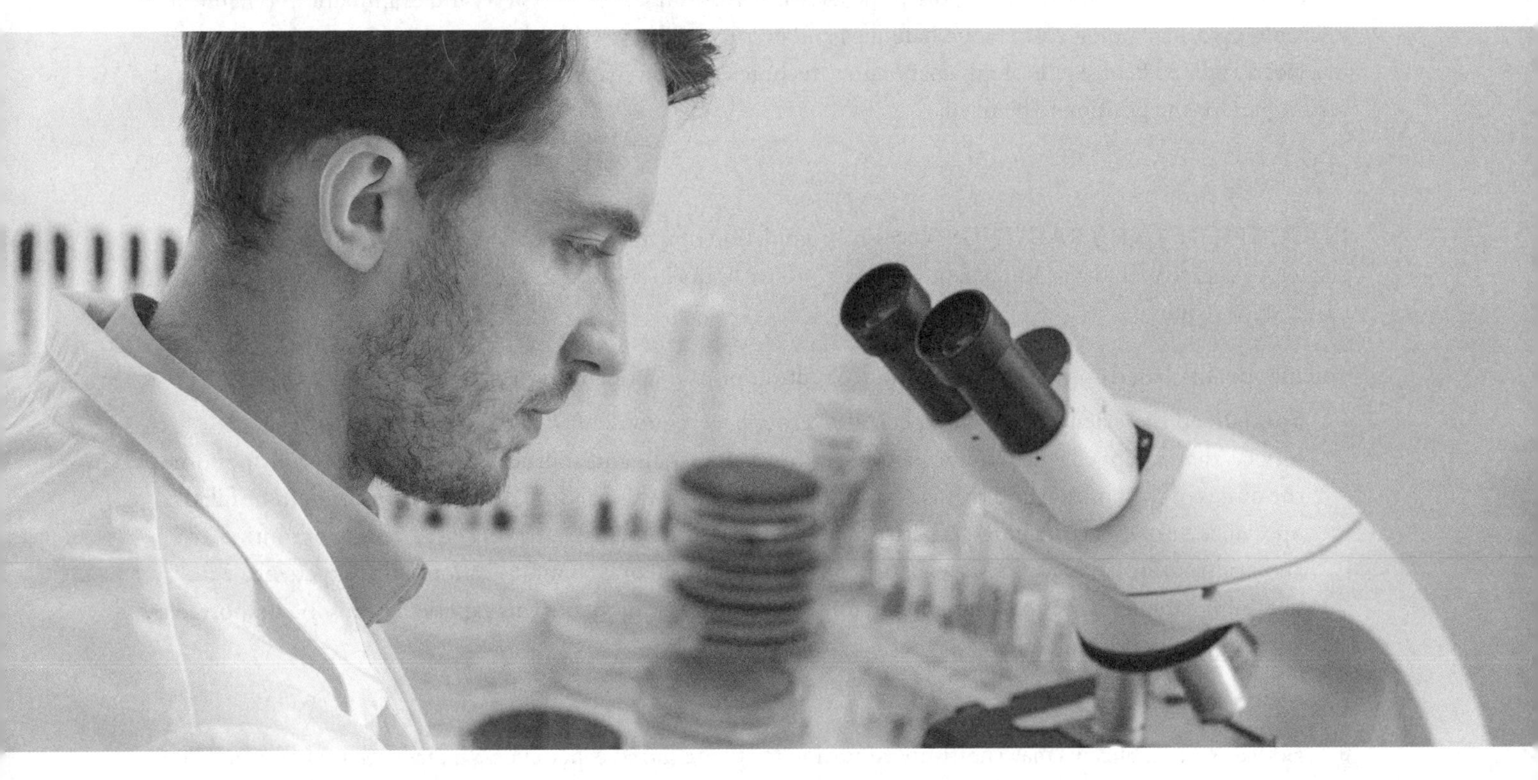

Hiring Authority: 30% or More Disabled Veteran, New Graduate

Current Job: US Army, Bioscience Research Technician, E-5

MOS: 68K—Medical Laboratory, Technician, July 2016 to Present

First Target Job: Veteran's Administration, Medical Technician, Pathology Services, GS-5

2nd Target Job Accepted: Science Research—Intern—Oak Ridge Institute for Science and Education (ORISE) (Government Contract Research)

Mike Kozlowski, Army Community Service Specialist (Employment) at Fort Rucker, AL, advised and coached Jonathan on his first Federal resume. Since Jonathan was a recent graduate, we added his education first on the resume with coursework. And his clinical technical skills were important for his Medical Technician target position.

RESULTS

Jonathan landed a contract position first, but applied for positions at MEDCOM and the VA for GS 5 positions.

BASIC REQUIREMENTS

(a) Technical medical laboratory support work such as performing laboratory tests and examinations (chemical, microbiologic, hematologic and blood banking) and preparing reports of findings or (b) technical support work in a closely related field, e.g., biological laboratory technician work, that required application of the methods and techniques for the position to be filled.

OR

EDUCATION AND TRAINING: Successful completion of a full 4-year course of study leading to a bachelor's degree with major study or at least 24 semester hours in subjects appropriate to the position to be filled (Transcript required).

You may qualify based on your experience and/or education as described below:

- **Specialized Experience:** 1-year of specialized experience, equivalent to the GS-04 level in the Federal service, that equipped you with the particular knowledge, skills and abilities needed to successfully perform the duties of the position and that is typically in or related to this Medical Technician position to be filled. Specialized experience includes: experience performing venipuncture; carrying out a variety of routine and non-routine laboratory tests; experience with written and oral communication skills; experience with obtaining samples; experience with maintaining laboratory equipment. This experience must be supported by your resume to be creditable.

OR

- **Education:** Applicants may substitute education for the required experience. To qualify based on education for this grade level you must have a 4-year course of study above high school leading to a bachelor's degree with courses related to the Medical Technician occupation.

You will be rated on the following Competencies for this position:

- Customer Service
- Follow Directions
- Patient Care
- Specimen Collection
- Standards
- Technical Competence

BEFORE AND AFTER KEYWORDS

BEFORE RESUME KEYWORDS

- BIOSCIENCE RESEARCH
- TECHNICIAN
- FORKLIFT DRIVER
- EMT-P
- GROUND SUPPORT EQUIPMENT
- SOFTWARE DEVELOPMENT
- AS, LABORATORY TECHNOLOGY
- AS, NURSING

AFTER KEYWORDS - *TARGETED*

- CLINICAL SKILLS
- BIOSCIENCE RESEARCH LABORATORY TECHNICIAN
- INJURY AND BIOMECHANICS PROTECTION GROUP
- HIPAA REGULATORY COMPLIANCE
- LITERATURE REVIEW
- BIOLOGICAL FLUIDS TESTING EXPERTISE
- CHEMISTRY
- HEMATOLOGY & COAGULATION
- MACROSCOPIC AND MICROSCOPIC URINALYSIS
- MICROORGANISM CULTURES SETUPS
- PHLEBOTOMY PRACTICES & PROCEDURES
- QUALITY CONTROL PROCESSES
- REPORTS OF FINDINGS

BEFORE AND AFTER ORGANIZATION

BEFORE RESUME ORGANIZATION

- OBJECTIVE
- KEY QUALIFICATIONS
- EXPERIENCE
- EDUCATION
- PROFESSIONAL DEVELOPMENT

AFTER RESUME ORGANIZATION

- CERTIFICATIONS
- EDUCATION AND COURSE LISTING
- TECHNICAL SKILLS
- WORK HISTORY (CLINICAL / US ARMY MILITARY LABORATORY AND HOSPITAL)
- PREVIOUS EXPERIENCE (NON-CLINICAL)

BEFORE RESUME

This resume is a bare-minimum resume, with no details of experience, no courses, no certifications, no Federal compliance details. This resume isn't even good for private sector job searches. This is too short.

Jonathan Craft

Email / phone

OBJECTIVE:

Detail-oriented IT support specialist seeking a position as a software developer to provide support within a rapidly growing technology company. Ability to install and troubleshoot Windows Operating Systems.

KEY QUALIFICATIONS:

Secret clearance
Python knowledge
Java knowledge
Multi tasker
years of experience

EXPERIENCE:

US Army **JULY 2016-PRESENT**
Bioscience Research Technician
Conducted chemical analysis of body fluids to determine abnormal components. Proficient in drawing blood for laboratory values. Knowledgeable in medical terminology.

Pactiv Corp, CANANDAIGUA, NY **JULY 2015- JULY 2017**
Forklift Driver
Perform required tasks operating appropriate equipment – clamp truck, sit down truck, stand up truck, slip sheet truck, barcode readers and safety equipment. Ability to train & certify employees on all powered industrial equipment in warehouse.

VIP Ambulance Services, SAN JUAN, PR **2013-2015**

EMT-P

Air One Maintenance, OPA LOCKA, FL **2010-2013**

Ground support equipment maintenance

EDUCATION AND PROFESSIONAL DEVELOPMENT:

- Bachelor's in Applied Software Development, Bellevue University, Nebraska, March 2021
- Associate in Science Laboratory Technology, George Washington University, May 2019, GPA: 3.61
- Associate in Science of Nursing, University of the Sacred Heart, PR, June 2015

Basic Leader Course 4 weeks May 2018

Cyber Awareness Training
Equal Opportunity and Anti-Harassment
Level 1 Antiterrorism Awareness
American Society of Clinical Pathologist certified

AFTER RESUME

A critical change in Jonathan's AFTER resume was moving education to the top, to emphasize his clinical technical skills.

Jonathan Craft
1000 Smith Street, Enterprise, AL 36330
444-444-4444 • Jcraft@aol.com
U.S. Army 5-Point Veteran Eligible Under VEOA
Current Secret Clearance (expires: 12-23-2026)

CERTIFICATIONS

Certified Medical Library Technician (CMLT), American Society for Clinical Pathology, 2016
Medical Laboratory Technician (MLT), Completed 52 weeks MLT course, US Army, 2016
EMT-Paramedic, South Eastern College, Miami Lakes, FL, May 2012

EDUCATION

Information Technology Coursework, 2012 to 2021
BELLEVUE UNIVERSITY, Bellevue, NE
- **Major:** Software Development; 75 credits completed

Associate's Degree, Health Science Laboratory Technology, May 2019
GEORGE WASHINGTON UNIVERSITY, Washington, D.C.
- **Relevant Coursework:** MLS 1070: Clinical Lab Rotation I; MLS 1071: Clinical Lab Rotation II; MLS 1081: Clinical Chemistry I; MLS 1082: Clinical Chemistry II; MLS 1083: Hematology I; MLS 1084: Hematology II; MLS 1085: Urinalysis and Body Fluids; MLS 1086: Clinical Immunology; MLS 1087: Blood Banking I; MLS 1088: Blood Banking II; MLS 1089: Clinical Microbiology I; MLS 1090: Clinical Microbiology II

Associate's Degree, Nursing Science, April 2015
UNIVERSITY OF THE SACRED HEART, San Juan, PR
- **Relevant Coursework:** BIO 101: Human Biology I; BIO 102: Human Biology II; BIO 204: Intro Microbiology; ENF 231: Pharmacology; QUI 108: General Chemistry; INF 105: Intro to Computers

TECHNICAL SKILLS

Clinical Skills (4 years full-time experience): Perform laboratory tests and examinations (chemical, microbiologic, hematologic and blood banking). Prepare reports of findings and technical support biological laboratory technician work as a Medical Technician.

Computers: Windows/Mac operating systems • Composite Health Care System (CHCS) • Microsoft® Office Software Applications (Word, Excel, PowerPoint, Outlook) • Cepheid-Trained in Sars-CoV2 Testing • Basic Life Support (BLS) • Basic knowledge of Java programming language • ASCP-certified • Bilingual (Spanish)

BIOSCIENCE RESEARCH LABORATORY TECHNICIAN, E-4 07/2017–present
US Army Aeromedical Research Laboratory, Fort Rucker, AL Hours per week: 40
Supervisor: John Doe, 333-333-3333, may contact

Soldier Scientist Mentorship: Hand-picked by the Research Administration Manager to participate in the U.S. Army Aeromedical Research Laboratory Soldier Scientist Program, led by the Science Program Administrator. Trained by leading scientists within the organization on the ethics, standards, and regulations for sound research.

BIOMECHANICS PROTECTION: Support 7+ primary investigators and 45+ personnel across 6 research teams. Collaborate with research scientists to prevent spinal injury and head trauma protocols. Conduct basic and applied research for systematic inquiries into a variety of subject matter related to biomechanics protection.

HIPAA REGULATORY COMPLIANCE: Guarantee adherence to Health Insurance Portability and Accountability Act (HIPAA) requirements by ensuring sensitive information and research are properly handled and stored in accordance with Federal regulations. Review processes and procedures for file storage, information-sharing, and sensitive information protection.

SCIENTIFIC RESEARCH: Utilize knowledge of scientific principles, methods, and tools of research to conduct systematic inquiries and literature searches for scientific and medical researchers. Conduct research using a range of databases to review scholarly publications on complex, scientific topics.

Key Accomplishment:

- Co-authored and presented a peer-reviewed scientific article, "Assessment of Aircrew Head Injury Protection After Helmet Liner Modifications." Selected to present findings in the 91st Scientific Meeting Research Conference for Aerospace Medicine and Human Performance (AsMA) in Atlanta, GA.

MEDICAL LABORATORY TECHNICIAN (MLT), E-4 02/2016–07/2017
Carl R Darnall Army Medical Center (CRDMC), Fort Hood, Hours per week: 40
TX Supervisor: Jane Smith, 777-777-7777, may contact

BIOLOGICAL FLUIDS TESTING EXPERTISE: Performed complex procedures in different areas, such as STAT/routine hematology, coagulation, chemistry, urinalysis, serology, immunoassays, blood bank, and microbiology testing in compliance of the College of American Pathologists (CAP) and SOPs. Determined specimen suitability and identified criteria for specimen rejection. Identified chemistry panels' tests and dilutions. Understands significance of analytes.

LABORATORY EQUIPMENT OPERATIONS: Operated and set up laboratory equipment, such as Abbot Analyzers, Microscan Walkaway 96, FilmArray Biofire, SOFIA, IQ200, microscope, centrifuge, and others. Maintained daily maintenance regimen and attended to basic trouble shooting issues. Performed user-level preventive maintenance, calibration, and troubleshooting on urine analyzers.

SPECIALIZED BIOLOGICAL PROCEDURES: Followed precaution standards and properly labeled specimens. Collected venous and capillary blood samples. Identified specimens with unique handling or transport requirements. Applied collection procedures and rejection criteria to the following tests: 24-hour urines, glucose tolerance tests, lipid panels, ammonia, bilirubin, and PKU. Applied quality control procedures, maintaining records using QC charts to ensure results fall within normal established ranges before releasing patient results.

REPORTS OF FINDINGS: Assessed and reported patients critical results utilizing CHCS/LIS. Applied the principles of EBVV/mononucleosis, hepatitis, HIV/HTLV, and MMR when reporting findings concerning the same. Identified and reported normal or abnormal colors and appearance of the urine specimens.

Key Accomplishments:

- ASCP: National certification obtained on first try. During fiscal year 2016, the exam was administered to 370 MLT students, with only a 74% passing rate. Less than 15% of Army-wide MLTs have attempted and passed this exam.
- MLT Training: Completed a 52-week MLT course with the US Army on first try. Currently hold the military enlisted occupational specialty (MOS) of medical laboratory technician.

FORKLIFT DRIVER 07/2014–02/2016
PACTIV CORPORATION, Canandaigua, NY Hours per week: 40

BASIC EQUIPMENT OPERATION: Performed required tasks operating appropriate equipment-clamp truck, sit down truck, stand up truck, slip sheet truck, barcode readers, and safety equipment.

EMPLOYEE TRAINING: Trained and certified employees on powered industrial equipment in warehouse. Ensured employees understood federal, state, and local guidelines on safe equipment operation.

PARAMEDIC 12/2012–07/2014
VIP Ambulance Services, Guaynabo, PR Hours per week: 40
Supervisor: Joe Hugh, 555-555-5555, may contact

BASIC/ADVANCED LIFE SUPPORT: Administered basic and advanced life support measures in accordance with established policies and procedures. Participated in other forms of emergency care and medical rescue.

INVASIVE MEDICAL PROCEDURES: Performed invasive medical procedures under delegated medical practice of a physician including venipuncture, airway management techniques such as endotracheal intubation, administration of intravenous fluids, and approved medications and defibrillation.

GLORIA HAYES
FEDERAL RESUME CASE STUDY #7

Hiring Authority: US Army Military Spouse and Recent Graduate

Current Position: Military Spouse / Legal Assistant

Target: Paralegal Specialist, Ft. Rucker Judge Advocate General's Office, Alabama, GS-7

Mike Kozlowski, Army Community Service Specialist *(Employment)* at Fort Rucker, AL, advised and coached Gloria on her first Federal resume. Gloria had been applying to Paralegal Federal positions with the BEFORE resume in this case study with no success. Never Best Qualified! For the new resume, since Gloria was a recent graduate, we added her education first with coursework. Her coursework and notary public certification were important. Her Military Spouse experience was important too, including her Key Spouse Duties for 4 years.

QUALIFICATIONS REQUIRED

QUALIFICATIONS

To be eligible at any of the grade levels defined below, you must meet at least ONE of the following conditions: Specialized Experience, Education, OR a Combination of Education and Experience.

FOR THE GS-07 LEVEL: Applicants must have one year of specialized experience (equivalent to the GS-05 level) that may have been obtained in the private or public (local, county, state, Federal) sectors which demonstrates:

Practical knowledge of a body of laws and related rules, regulations, and precedents involved in Federal employee appeals and litigation relating to Federal employment.

Skill in interpreting and applying them to varying situations; skill in evaluating the relevancy of precedents and summarizing pertinent data on issues.

Skill in problem analysis and problem solving sufficient to communicate in the style and mode appropriate for work at the level of an appeals court.

How You Will Be Evaluated

- Knowledge of research, including electronic research, interpretation, and application of case law relating to employment law.
- Skill in using an electronic case management system to enter, update, and maintain data to ensure that agency employees and managers have available accurate information related to status and history of each case.
- Ability and skill in reviewing and preparing a variety of legal documents

EDUCATION SUBSTITUTION FOR THE GS-07: Applicants may qualify based upon the completion of 1 full year of graduate level education or superior academic achievement leading to such a degree in a closely related field as Paralegal Studies or Legal Studies. Equivalent combinations of education and experience are qualifying for this grade level.

BEFORE AND AFTER KEYWORDS

BEFORE RESUME KEYWORDS

- LEGAL ASSISTANT
- PARALEGAL

AFTER KEYWORDS - *TARGETED*

- PARALEGAL STUDIES AAS
- NOTARY PUBLIC
- MILTIARY KEY SPOUSE
- LEGAL ASSISTANT (ADMINISTRATIVE LAW)
- LEGAL FILES
- LEGAL WRITTEN COMMUNICATIONS
- SYSTEMS PROFICIENCY
- LEGAL RESEARCH

BEFORE AND AFTER ORGANIZATION

BEFORE RESUME ORGANIZATION

- OBJECTIVE
- SKILLS
- EXPERIENCE
- EDUCAT

AFTER RESUME ORGANIZATION

- MILITARY SPOUSE PREFERENCE
- EDUCATION AND COURSE LISTING
- LICENSES AND CERTIFICATIONS
- WORK HISTORY
- MILITARY SPOUSE
- LEGAL ASSISTANT
- PARALEGAL

BEFORE RESUME

This resume is a bare-minimum resume, with no details of experience, no courses, no certifications, no Federal compliance details. This resume isn't even good for private sector job searches. This is too short.

Gloria Hayes

100 Redhat Way
Enterprise, Alabama 36330
999-999-9999 | gloriahayes@gmail.com

Objective

Seeking an opportunity that will allow me to demonstrate that I am a hard-working individual who is anxious to increase my knowledge, and utilize my experience thereby becoming an asset to the office.

Skills

I am a team player who works well with others. My strong communication skills are I speak both English and Spanish. I have extensive customer service experience working in a high stress and high-volume office. I enjoy a challenge and putting my education and experience to use.

Experience

Staff Judge Advocacy — **Fort Rucker, Alabama**
Legal Assistant — **August 2019 to Present**

- Notarizing Powers of Attorney's and Wills
- Drafting Powers of Attorney's Custom to Needs of families and Soldiers
- Administrative Duties
- Assisted in drafting letters for Tort Claims
- Assist in training of incoming Soldiers

Staff Judge Advocacy — **Fort Rucker, Alabama**
Paralegal — **Sep 2018 to August 2019**

- Maintain files
- Assisting in Drafting of Correspondence
- Learned on the job Training

Education:

Currently attending Enterprise State Community College for my Associates in Paralegal Studies

Projected graduation August of 2019 — Member of the National Honor Society

Paralegal Student of The Year — President's List Fall 2018

AFTER RESUME

In the AFTER resume, Gloria's education comes first as she is a recent graduate. It also features her certification as a Notary and her Military Spouse experience.

GLORIA HAYES

100 Redhat Way · Enterprise, AL 36330
999-999-9999 gloriahayes@gmail.com

MILITARY SPOUSE PREFERENCE

Eligible for consideration under Executive Order 13473
Noncompetitive Appointment for Certain Military Spouse

EDUCATION

Associate of Science (AAS), Paralegal Studies — **08/2019**
Enterprise State Community College, Enterprise, Alabama

Microcomputer Applications
Domestic Relations Law
Wills, Estates, and Trusts
Legal and Social Environment of Business
Basic and Advanced Legal Research and Writing
Civil Law and Procedures
Law Office Management
Introduction to Real Property Law

LICENSES AND CERTIFICATIONS

STATE OF ALABAMA NOTARY PUBLIC, Bond # 5005324 Expiration 01/14/2023

PROFESSIONAL EXPERIENCE

Military Spouse of an Active Duty US Army Soldier — **08/2006 to present**
20 hours per week

Fort Rucker, AL	2017–Present
Hunter Army Airfield, Savannah, GA	2013–2017
Fort Rucker, AL	2011–2013
Fort Bliss, TX	2009–2011
Fort Benning, GA	2006–2009

Key Spouse **1/2017 to present**
Army Community Center, Ft. Rucker, AL 20 hours per week
Volunteer

KNOWLEDGEABLE OF INSTALLATION AGENCIES AND COMMUNITY SERVICES: Single Point of Contact for 125+ arriving and departing military and civilian members and their spouses for information on family advocacy programs, healthcare, childcare, and education services. Participate in unit and spouses' group functions and meetings. Deliver peer-to-peer support cultivating relationships within the spousal network. Organize unit events and contribute to squadron Hails & Farewells, squadron functions, spouses' group functions, and Airmen and Family Readiness Center meetings and training.

ORAL AND WRITTEN COMMUNICATIONS: Brief Squadron personnel, leadership, members, and families of the Key Spouse program on services and program functions. Create pocket contact card with key unit personnel, installation numbers, and newcomer's welcome process. Address new members' questions about installation procedures and coordinate with others to assist families during deployment or on temporary assignment. Track and maintain unit family call logs, record action taken, and provide advice regarding family readiness issues. Draft emails, correspondence, newsletters, and policy letters.

IMPLEMENT SOCIAL SERVICE PROGRAMS: Collaborate with unit leadership to analyze current and future members' needs. Outline support services for Key Spouse program, and develope special events, marketing pamphlets, and a program education briefing for leadership.

ORGANIZE, DEVELOP, AND COORDINATE PROGRAM GOALS AND OBJECTIVES: Collaborate with Unit Commander to outline goals and direction of Key Spouse program. To promote program goals and establish brand recognition, created a social media site, monthly newsletter, and newcomer's welcome kit. Coordinate workshops for families on finances, employment, and parenting. Supported and executed 5 volunteer and morale events with a budget of $10K and overall attendance of 1,200.

COUNSEL, ADVISE, AND ASSIST CLIENTS WITH LIFE ISSUES: Advise spouses and dependents while service members are away at training or deployment. Assisted 50 members with community programs regarding family advocacy, employment opportunities.

Legal Assistant (Administrative Law) **08/2019–Present**
OFFICE OF THE STAFF JUDGE ADVOCATE 30 hours per week (average)
Building 5700, Fort Rucker, AL
Supervisor: Mr. Christopher R. Kelley, (334) 111-1111; may contact

LEGAL FILES AND REPORTS MANAGEMENT: Maintain legal office files for 3 to 5 attorneys in accordance with Army Records Information Management System (ARIMS). Maintain reports. Enter, transcribe, record, and maintain information in written or electronic form. Maintain order of legal documents in accordance with established office protocols.

LEGAL WRITTEN COMMUNICATIONS: Review correspondence and documents to determine nature of action(s) requested. Comply with standardized office procedures, instructions, and pertinent regulations. Compose routine correspondence as needed from brief notes, emails, and oral instructions. Assist the Client Service Division if needed by notarizing legal documentation.

ELECTRONIC SYSTEMS PROFICIENCY: Experienced in Microsoft Office 2016 software applications (Word, Excel, and Outlook). Regularly access Army Knowledge Online (AKO), Judge Advocacy

General Corps Network (JAGCNET), and Administrative Law Case System database (ALCS) for record and data collection.

LEGAL RESEARCH: Research applicable regulations or laws in accordance with specific cases as requested by legal center attorneys. Write legal deposition summaries and discoveries. Write legal motions and complaints as directed by staff attorneys.

KEY ACCOMPLISHMENTS:

- Took the initiative to request a transfer to the administrative law department to learn the legal assistance position, gaining the confidence of the staff attorney team to perform the job in an unsupervised environment.
- Volunteered to take on several roles normally expected of a paralegal. These included (but were not limited to) creating deposition summaries and case filings for the staff attorneys. I received "kudos" for my superlative efforts.
- Completed 300 hours of volunteer service hours in 2 different legal departments, while performing general administrative duties. I learned different skill sets vital to the job and exceeded all staff attorneys' expectations.

Paralegal, Legal Assistance Division **09/2018–08/2019**
OFFICE OF THE STAFF JUDGE ADVOCATE
Building 5700, Fort Rucker, AL 36362 34 hours per week (average)
Supervisor: John Calahan (573) 555-5555; may contact:

LEGAL ADMINISTRATIVE SUPPORT: Provided customer and client services as well as general administrative support to 5 attorneys and the Chief of Staff of Legal Assistance. Composed routine correspondence. Screened telephone calls to determine the appropriate legal issue involved, making initial assignments of cases.

ELECTRONIC SYSTEMS PROFICIENCY: Experienced in Microsoft office 2016 software applications (Word, Excel, and Outlook). Regularly accessed AKO and JAGCNET. Maintained database for all Soldier and Family Law attorney staff with JAGCNET and the CIS. Hardware qualified: copy machine, CAC scanner, fax, telephone, printer.

CLIENT SERVICES: Answered telephone calls and distributed messages to appropriate attorney staff members. Scheduled client appointments based on the needs of soldiers and families and staff attorney availability. Notarized wills and powers of attorney as needed. Drafted powers of attorney and other forms that were authorized for notarization through the installation of the Army.

KEY ACCOMPLISHMENTS:

- I successfully learned skills in 2 different departments with a total of 9 different attorneys and 2 different Chiefs of Staff on 2 different systems vital to administrative law and legal assistance reports maintenance.
- I proposed improvements for scheduling conflict resolutions, which were approved by staff attorneys. These systems tracked clients who may have had conflicts of interest when it came to divorce appointments. This resulted in a greater degree of confidentiality between the disputing parties, enhancing conflict resolution.
- I implemented an appointment resolution binder to accommodate those who needed appointments for wills and were not able to be accommodated immediately.

RESULTS Gloria landed her targeted position!

STEP 7

WRITE YOUR ACCOMPLISHMENTS

It's time to brag! One of the most important parts of a successful Federal resume is the description of your major accomplishments at work. USAJOBS announcements usually require specialized experience in a particular area. Many times, they will ask for examples that demonstrate this specialized experience. The best way to demonstrate your specialized experience, and get Best Qualified or Referred to a supervisor, is with accomplishments that prove your excellent performance and value to your organization. It is important to separate your overall duties and responsibilities from your major achievements on the job. Preparing for an interview also requires getting ready to describe job-related accomplishments.

What is the best way to write up your top 10 accomplishments?
The Office of Personnel Management has a recommended format for writing KSAs and your accomplishments record in a story-telling format: the Context, Challenge, Action, Result (CCAR) Model for writing better KSAs. This CCAR story-telling format is also great for the Behavior-Based Interview.

CONTEXT

The context should include the role you played in this example. Were you a team member, planner, organizer, facilitator, administrator, or coordinator? Also, include your job title at the time and the timeline of the project. You may want to note the name of the project or situation.

CHALLENGE

What was the specific problem that you faced that needed resolution? Describe the challenge of the situation. The problem could be disorganization in the office, new programs that needed to be implemented or supported, a change in management, a major project stalled, or a large conference or meeting being planned. The challenge can be difficult to write about. You can write the challenge last when you are drafting your KSAs.

ACTION

What did you do that made a difference? Did you change the way the office processed information, responded to customers, managed programs? What did you do?

RESULT

What difference did it make? Did this new action save dollars or time? Did it increase accountability and information? Did the team achieve its goals?

Use our free CCAR Accomplishment Builder!
www.resume-place.com/resources/ccar-builder/

Top 10 List of Accomplishments for Cedrick Smith
Target: GS-0303-8, Technical Operations Group Assistant

1. The USS ZUMWALT was commissioned in Baltimore, MD in 2016. As the first sole administrative officer for the ship in 2017, I performed all administrative matters alone for a year.
2. After one year, I successfully submitted justifications and requests to expand our manpower and was able to add two more personnel to the Administrative team supporting 160 sailors on the ship.
3. The ship deployed many times. I administered complete tests of the ship's capabilities.
4. For initial recruitment, I successfully collaborated with Military Enlisted & Officer personnel, Federal Civilians & Contractors, and transferring service members from the Navy / Air Force Pacific for the ship's administrative operations.
5. Instrumental in the retention of personnel to ensure proper manning levels were maintained for ZUMWALT and the US Navy.
6. Oversaw all aspects of the personnel security program, utilizing JPAS/DISS to initiate, update, and close out personnel security investigations and visit requests.
7. Managed a $100K travel budget to ensure that the agency maintained the appropriate number of specially trained personnel on board. Coordinated flight and lodging requests for personnel and ensured proper account reconciliation after the completion of travel.
8. As President of the Morale Welfare & Recreation Committee, I marshalled a 12-person team through the organization of multiple crew-focused events and tournaments, sourcing of new gym equipment, and the 2019 Spring Picnic and Command Holiday party, uplifting crew morale and generating over $12K to support the welfare of the ZUMWALT and her crew.
9. Established document and records management policies and processes for the 160 sailors on the ship. Ensured all personal data within the command's records system was safeguarded in accordance with the DoD Privacy Act.
10. As the program coordinator, I ensured that all unmarried sailors with children had an approved family care plan on file to ensure quality of life for the sailors on board the ship.

KSAS

Many announcements include KSAs. You will need to demonstrate these KSAs in the resume—maybe as an accomplishment!

KSAs stands for KNOWLEDGE, SKILLS, and ABILITIES.

Example KSA language from a vacancy announcement:

Knowledge, Skills and Abilities

Possess at least one year of specialized experience performing work of the type listed in the following examples:

- developing, preparing, and presenting terms and conditions in bids or proposals related to the award of contracts
- or negotiating and awarding contracts, contract modifications, and subcontract
- or in legal practice involving the analysis of procurement policies and procedures
- or administering the terms and conditions of contracts including such aspects as preparing contract modifications

For Federal job applications, you must pay attention that you demonstrate that you have the required KSAs.

Where to demonstrate KSAS:

Resume work experience sections
Resume accomplishments
Questionnaire narrative questions
Questionnaire multiple choice questions
Interview

NOTE: If you have a Top 10 List of Accomplishments, these accomplishments will probably match the KSAs!

TWO CCAR ACCOMPLISHMENTS

CCAR Example 1

See how to write a CCAR accomplishment story. Use this narrative in an interview or for the questionnaire. You can also use this in your resume in the longer form or shorten if needed.

Challenge: Client information was tracked in folders, which led to lapses in insurance, loss of coverage, and thousands of dollars lost.

Context: Case Manager, Ridgeland Office, June 2018 to November 2019

Action:
1. Researched and learned advanced Microsoft Excel formulas that allowed for the most efficient alert system.
2. Researched insurance procedures to determine the time parameters needed to create a functional system.
3. Trained co-workers on the system, which allowed the integration of the software into other departments.

Results: The formulated tracking software allowed medical records to be alerted to clients' lapse dates and improved re-authorization procedures to save the client from being removed from services as well as save the company ~$20,000/month through drastically reduced instances of denied insurance coverage.

CCAR Example 2

Another example of a CCAR story to use in the resume, interview, or narrative questions.

Challenge: The original plan for Month of the Military Child celebration was cancelled due to COVID-19. I had to short notice come up with a new plan to celebrate MOMC while battling the social distancing restrictions.

Context: Airman & Family Readiness Program Manager, April 1-30, 2020

Action:
1. I had to get creative and come up with a new plan to engage children and families while adhering to the social distancing restrictions. Battling short notice on the change of plans and dealing with the stressors of COVID-19. Found a way to host a contest with no cost associated with the event.
2. Worked with a graphic designer to create a design specifically for Kingsley Field. Coordinated with Public Affairs to promote the coloring contest and also promoted Resiliency resources in addition to hosting the contest.
3. Created social media account for the A&FRC to promote contest and increase client reach virtually.

Results: Resulted in over 60 child participants from the local area. The outcome and participation were so well received and positive that Brigadier General for the Oregon Air National Guard acknowledged and announced contest winner live via Facebook to the entire ORANG.

ACCOMPLISHMENTS: BEFORE AND AFTER

Highlighting Projects with Accomplishments

Here is an example of how including projects with accomplishments takes a resume from ordinary to exceptional.

Before (just a laundry list):

INFORMATION TECHNOLOGY FIELD SERVICE TECHNICIAN (NETWORK): Install, troubleshoot, test, splice, repair, and maintain telephone equipment and general network equipment, customer premise equipment, Video/CATV/DBS, fiber optic/copper facilities and/or other TDS products and services for new and existing customers. Install, configure, maintain, and repair Key Systems, PBX, Centrex Systems, and other business systems such as fiber terminals, ISPs, ISDN, DSL, T-1s, and/or DS3s (carriers, paging, and wireless). Provide high level support for enhancing and maintaining record systems (cross connects, line groups, network elements, etc.).
Provide excellent customer service. Proactively educate and sell TDS products and services to customers.
Perform project management of the installation of systems and perform related functions as requested by supervisor.
Utilize databases, Trouble/Repair/Dispatch Systems, Plant Record Systems, MS Outlook, MS Word, MS Excel, MS Explorer, and CD-ROMs.

After (very impressive):

TDS Telecom, Cyril, OK 73029
Information Technology Field Service Technician (Network)

TECHNICAL SUPPORT FOR COMPUTER SOFTWARE AND HARDWARE ISSUES
Install, troubleshoot, repair, and maintain telecommunications products and equipment that TDS sells and leases (Routers, Switches, Hubs, Calix Systems, Key Systems, and/or other business systems).

MAKE RECOMMENDATIONS AND/OR SYSTEM MODIFICATIONS
Direct, face-to-face contact with customers and expected to be proactive with the sales of TDS services and products. Services include, but are not limited to Telephony, Internet, and/or High-Speed Networks.

RESOLVE PROBLEM RECURRENCE
Provide hardware and software installation and troubleshooting for customers in multiple locations including Cyril, Fletcher, Elgin, and Apache, OK.

Key Projects

- Team Lead for a seven-member Help Desk Team providing support to 300 end-users assisting disaster relief operations after a local storm created an Internet outage. Resulted in increased communication to customers and decreased downtime for network services.
- Maintained network and improved efficiency by 42% using PDCA Framework-Plan, Do, Check, Act. Developed two new work process flows for installation of services, had to use Anova T and Z tests to see which one would provide the most results in increased efficiency. Provided continuous improvement and monitoring of organization network for the CIO.
- Implemented network management processes for senior management keeping them informed of efficiency, risk, and customer service business objectives. Created a new Standard Operating Procedure (SOP) for help desk employees to utilize during customer trouble calls. Resulted in reducing the process lead time for customer service requests by 38%.

ACCOMPLISHMENTS: BEFORE AND AFTER

Reworking the Job Block

Here is an example of how working the accomplishments into your job block can turn an ordinary list of duties into a star potential candidate for a position.

Before:

CUSTOMER SERVICE: Initial point of contact for Army Community Service (ACS) at Fort Meade. Explain ACS programs and work life related services to approximately 100 community members on the phone and in person daily. Listen to needs of customers and provide referral services to Service members, Family members, Retirees, and Civilians. Resolve conflicts and ensure course of action is effective in meeting client's needs. Follow appropriate routing procedures when solution needs to be found by supervisor.

After (very impressive):

Recipient: Excellence in Federal Career Award Winner, Silver and Gold for the following significant contributions to the Ft. Meade Army Community Service

DEVELOPED MISSION-CRITICAL STATISTICS FOR PROGRAM EVALUATION: Independently took online courses on how to develop a wide variety of graphs, charts and worksheets to capture important and useful statistics regarding Visitor Center use. This information has been instrumental in the strategic planning process for the center and is utilized in high visibility briefings, slides and reports to demonstrate usage, trends and impact. During the center's triennial accreditation inspection, my data products received the highest accolades from the inspectors and were heralded as benchmarks for ACS Centers worldwide to emulate.

IMPROVED CUSTOMER SERVICE: Redesigned the lobby and reception area to make the space more professional and appealing to ACS customers. Quickly recognized that many customers needed detailed information about the installation, so I researched and ordered a large map of the post. My initiative had an immediate and dramatic impact on customer service. It provided clients a great tool that was understandable and easily accessible. Furthermore, by decreasing the need for customers to be shown a small map at the front desk, it increased the amount of time that can be spent on customers with more critical needs.

NOTE: Federal Resume Accomplishments will help you get **Referred, Interviewed, and Hired!**

ACCOMPLISHMENTS: BEFORE AND AFTER

Education Accomplishments

If you need to highlight your education, see how adding the accomplishment information improves the resume.

Before: Bachelor of Science - Media Arts in Digital Video Production - Platt College, San Diego, April 2020

After: BACHELOR OF SCIENCE, Media Arts in Digital Video Production • April 2020 • Platt College • San Diego, CA • GPA: 3.88 • Relevant Coursework: Reporting & Writing the News, Documentary Process, Broadcast Journalism, Media Computer Graphics, Broadcast Production, Advertising in Mass Media, Interpersonal Communication, Mass Media Law.

ACADEMIC PROJECTS

LANDSCAPE AND PORTRAIT PHOTOGRAPHY: Utilized scouting techniques to determine best location to photograph subjects. Ensured every effort was taken to meet the criteria for project assignment. Used safety checklist to ensure shoot was within safety standards. Conducted research to determine the legality of location photography and filed correct forms when appropriate.

AUDIO VISUAL DESIGN: Created mini documentary on the operating procedures of street canvassers working with the Save the Children organization. Conducted numerous meetings with office managers and directors reviewing project logistics. Ensured correct legal paperwork was filed, such as release forms and Hold Harmless agreements. Used Creative Cloud to edit picture and sound.

STEP 7

COVER LETTERS

Cover letters are usually optional. In USAJOBS, you can add the letter into the Additional Information section or upload the cover letter into your USAJOBS account. Be sure to mention special considerations, such as your willingness to move or non-competitive hiring eligibilities. Highlight compelling reasons for considering your application.

This sample was created using the Resume Place FREE Cover Letter Builder:
www.resume-place.com/resources/cover-letter-builder/

JOHN SMITH
1000 Smith Avenue | Ft. McCoy, WI 90210
444-444-4444 | john.smith@gmail.com

June 5, 2021
Department Name
Address

RE: USAJOBS Announcement #: XXX-XXXX-XXX

To Whom It May Concern:

Please accept my resume and supporting materials in application for the Geospatial Analyst position with the National Geospatial Intelligence Agency (USAJOBS Announcement #: XXX-XXXX-XXX).

My relevant experience for the position includes:

- Three years of experience in military geospatial intelligence environments with in-depth work in map design, map production, and geospatial intelligence support.
- I have collaborated with entities such as U.S. Central Command, U.S. Cyber Command, and the Intelligence Community.
- I am a subject matter expert in cartography, including 3D modeling, and am fluent in the use of geospatial analysis and mapping software.

I believe that I would be an asset to your organization because:

- I have delivered high-quality geospatial support for several agencies within the Intelligence Community. I possess overseas military experience, including in support of active combat operations.
- My military record demonstrates that I am a skilled analyst and briefer with substantial real-world experience. I am known for my ability to communicate, to pull long hours, and for my precision in overseeing collection and mapping efforts.
- I am committed to providing rapid analyses and quality recommendations regardless of situational complexity. I will bring those skill sets and problem solving qualities to bear on NGA's challenges.

Thank you for your time and consideration. I look forward to your response.
Sincerely,
John Smith
Enclosures: Resume, DD-214

COVER LETTER SAMPLE 1 FOR NON-COMPETITIVE POSITIONS

NOTE: This is a Schedule A Cover Letter for the Selective Placement Program Manager.

From: Troy S. Yates
2220 Marcos Ave.
San Marcos, California 92078
E-mail: Troy.s.yates@gmail.com Home Phone: 888-888-8888
Work Phone: 888-888-8888

To: Rodney Leonard, Veteran's Representative Dept. of Homeland Security, Vets@dhs.gov

4/1/2021

Dear Mr. Leonard,

Please find enclosed my Federal Resume for the DHS positions in the areas of: Logistics Management Specialist, Emergency Management Specialist, Program Analysis and/or Administrative Officer. I would like to be considered for GS-11 or 12 positions. I am qualified for VRA, 30% or more Disabled, and Schedule A hiring programs.

My relevant experience for the above positions includes:

- 23 years of experience serving as an Officer in the U.S. Air Force. I was promoted to and served for 5 years in the top 4 percent of the entire U.S. Air Force total force structure. Uncompromising ethics and trustworthiness have been the cornerstones of my career.
- I have extensive experience as a Squadron Commander (Director) leading, managing, and overseeing the activities and operations of large, dynamic, and progressive organizations.
- As the Chief of Mission Assurance for the U.S. Air Force in the Pentagon, Washington DC, I'm experienced with senior level staff work developing and implementing policy requiring a collaborative, diplomatic, and political mindset.

I believe that I would be an asset to your organization because:

- I am highly detailed and bring an extensive knowledge of the principles and practices of supervision, organizational management, budgeting, administration, and personnel management.
- As a Servant Leader, I would develop and maintain a good-natured and engaging work environment for both the staff and community.

Sincerely, Troy S. Yates

Enclosures: DD-214, VA Letter and Schedule A Letter; 4-page Federal Resume

COVER LETTER SAMPLE 2 FOR NON-COMPETITIVE POSITIONS

NOTE: This is a Schedule A Cover Letter for Financial Management Analyst.

Dear Mr or Ms. xxxx:

I am reaching out to you as the Selective Placement Program Coordinator (SPPC) for the Department of the Navy to gain your advice regarding my applications for positions within the Department of the Navy under the Schedule A hiring authority. I am including a copy of my Schedule A qualification letter from my physician as well as my resume. I believe I am fully eligible for employment under the disability selective placement program and would appreciate any assistance you can provide me with the application process.

First, let me introduce myself. I have qualifications and experience in both the Financial Management and Information Technology fields. I am a U.S. Marine Corps Veteran (1999-2006) and during that period worked in positions of progressive responsibility as a Financial Management Resource Analyst. After leaving the Corps, I had several financial management positions, including over seven years of experience as the Accounting Administrator for Butler Home Services in Tucson, Arizona (2007-2015), in which I was the sole accounting manager for a home maintenance contracting firm, providing Accounts Payable/Accounts Receivable (AP/AR), payroll, contract management, and financial reporting functions. After moving to Ohio for family management reasons, I completed a boot camp in computer programming and have been successful in my resulting position (06/2019-Present) with IBM as an application developer. My resume (attached) provides more details of these positions.

I recently applied for the position as Financial Management Analyst with the Department of the Navy (Announcement # DE-10636178-20-AA), which required that applicants have the following experience to qualify as a GS-9: (1) Applying regulations, policies, and operating instructions applicable to financial management systems operations; (2) Identifying, analyzing and resolving a range of budgetary problems such as development of alternative methods of funding; and (3) Utilizing a variety of office automation software (word processing, presentation, spreadsheet, graphics, databases) to support financial management initiatives. My over seven years of experience as an Accounting Administrator for Butler Home Services (2007-2015) fully meets this requirement.

I am hoping that I have that combination of financial and leadership skills that would contribute to the Department of the Navy mission and would be open to any position where I could make a significant contribution to the organization.

I would very much appreciate your insight and any assistance you could provide me in navigating through the application process under the Schedule A hiring authority. I look forward to a personal interview to explain my qualifications in further detail. I am excited about the possibility of evolving my career into this next phase.

Please feel free to contact me with any further questions you have.

Sincerely,
Dominic Than
(777) 777-7777
DT171@gmail.com

Enclosures: DD-214, VA Letter and Schedule A Letter; 5-page Federal Resume

STEP 8
APPLY FOR THE JOB!

Applying for a Federal job on USAJOBS is surprisingly difficult, and it takes more effort and time than most people expect. Many people find this to be the second hardest step after writing your Federal resume. We highly recommend that you apply AT LEAST one day before the deadline.

Top problems people have with applying correctly:

- The person applied for a job that they are not eligible for.
- The resume does not show the Specialized Experience for the position.
- The Questionnaire does not give all the credit possible for the position, and the score is below the cut-off.
- Documents are missing.

Plan ahead! Setting up your account will take at least 1 hour, and the Resume Builder will take 1 to 2 hours to complete (after your resume has been drafted).

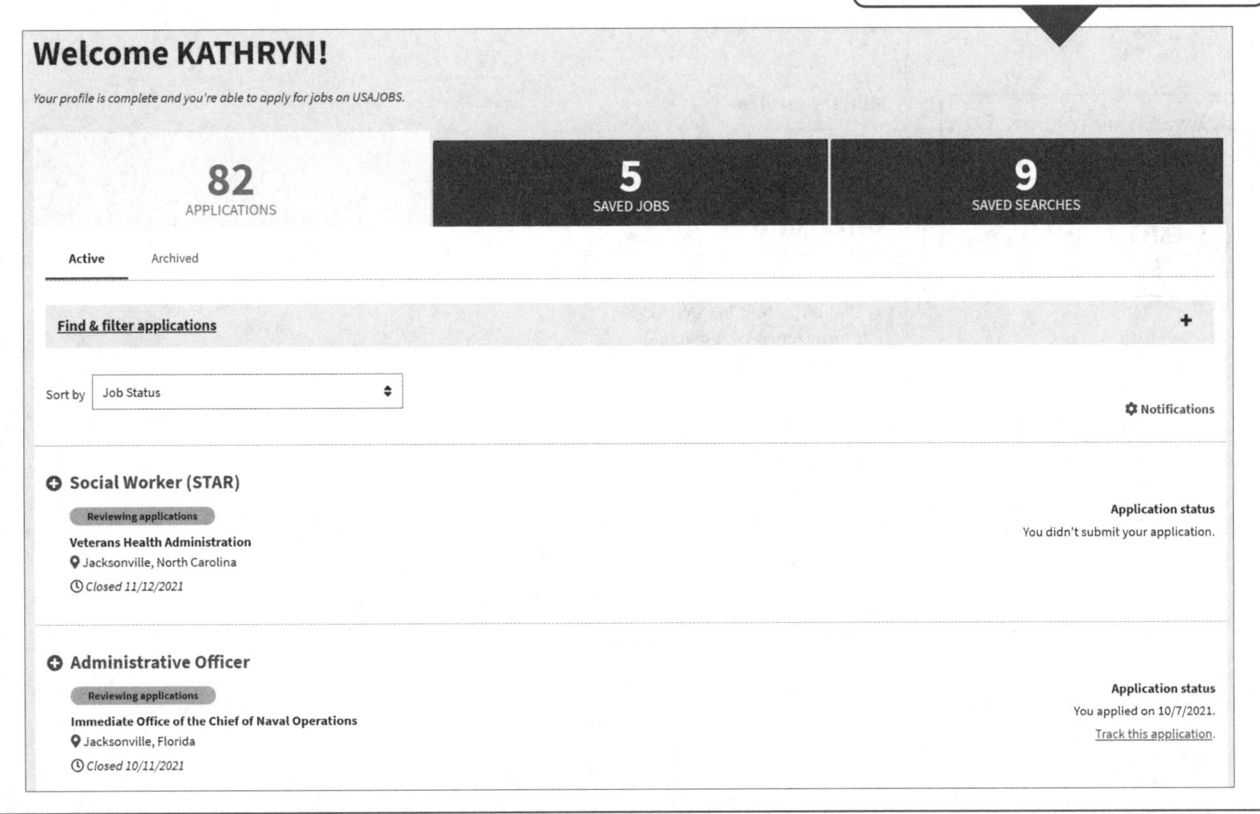

PART ONE: SET UP YOUR USAJOBS ACCOUNT

1. Go to *www.usajobs.gov*
2. Log in or create your account.
3. Click on the **Profile** tab and complete the items on this page.

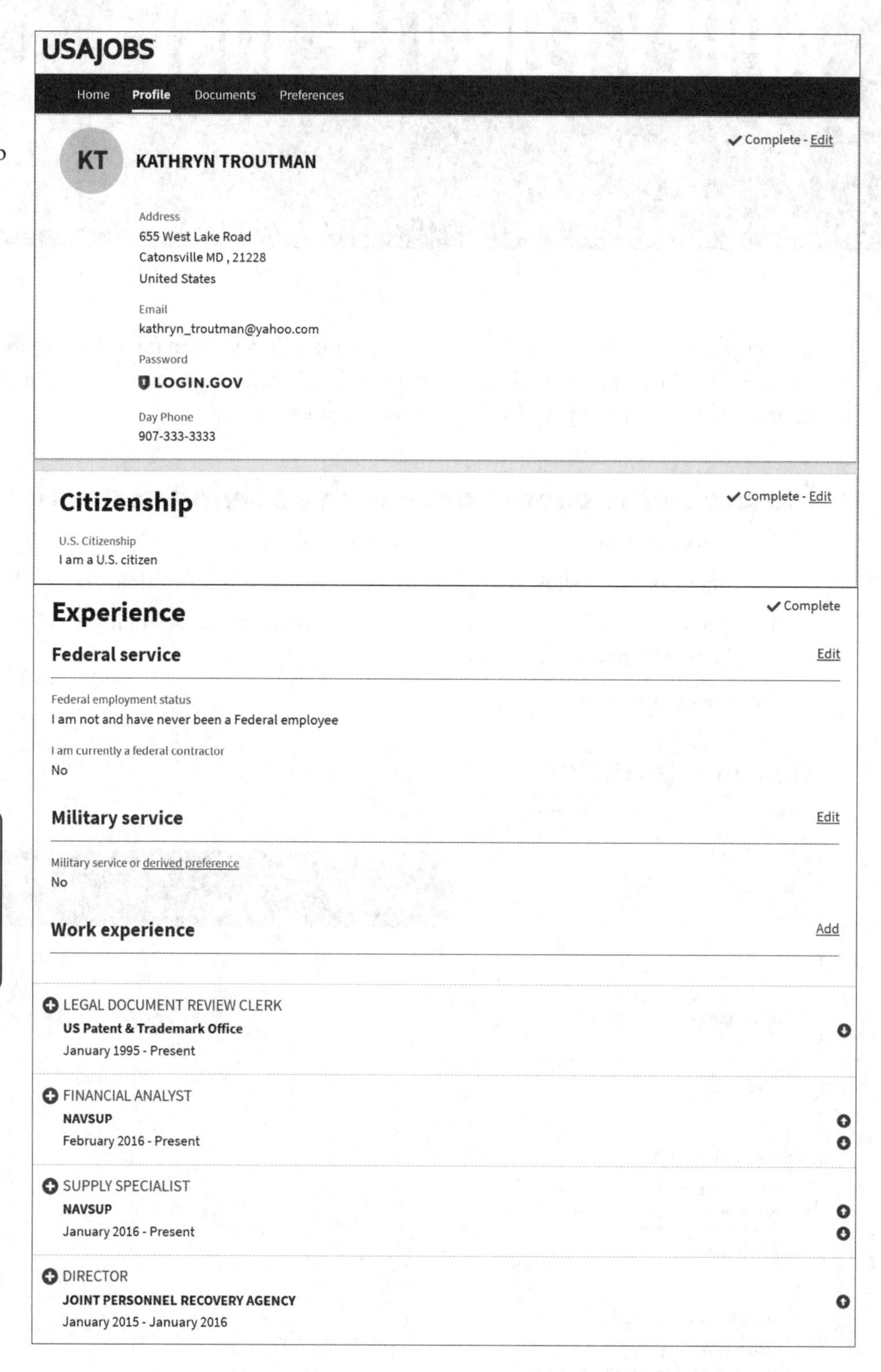

Be aware that resume information in your profile is searchable for resume mining! Update this information as needed for best results.

RESUME

Question: Should you use the Resume Builder or upload your resume?
Answer: BOTH!

First, build your resume in the Resume Builder. Some announcements are requiring that the resume be built using the Resume Builder. Also, using the Resume Builder will show you which information is required on your resume.

To create an UPLOAD format from the Resume Builder, just PRINT PREVIEW your resume. Copy it out and paste it into a WORD format. And then check the type font and spaces. Make the resume 11 point type with .75 inch margins. And then you can UPLOAD this resume.

When you are ready to build or upload your resume, click Documents > Resumes.

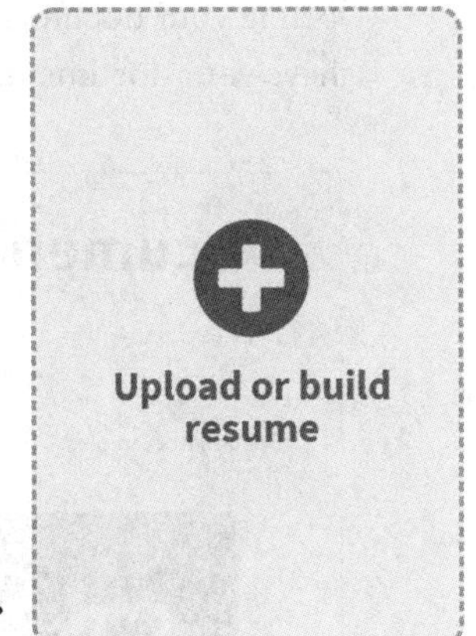

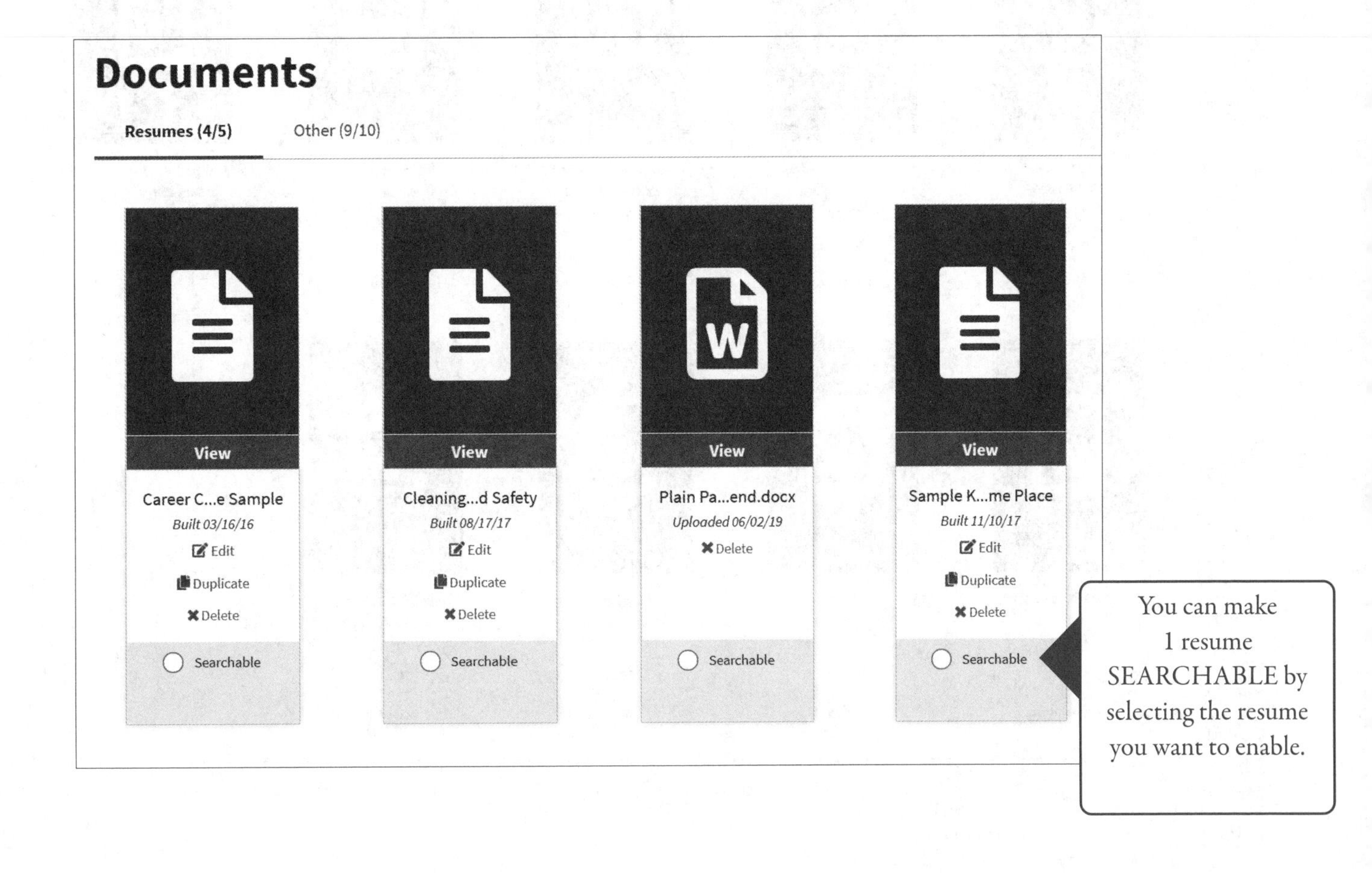

DOCUMENTS

When you are ready to upload additional documents, go to **Documents > Other.**

Name your documents correctly for their type so that they are recognized in the application system. Be sure to have your documents prepared ahead of time based on your eligibility for the position.

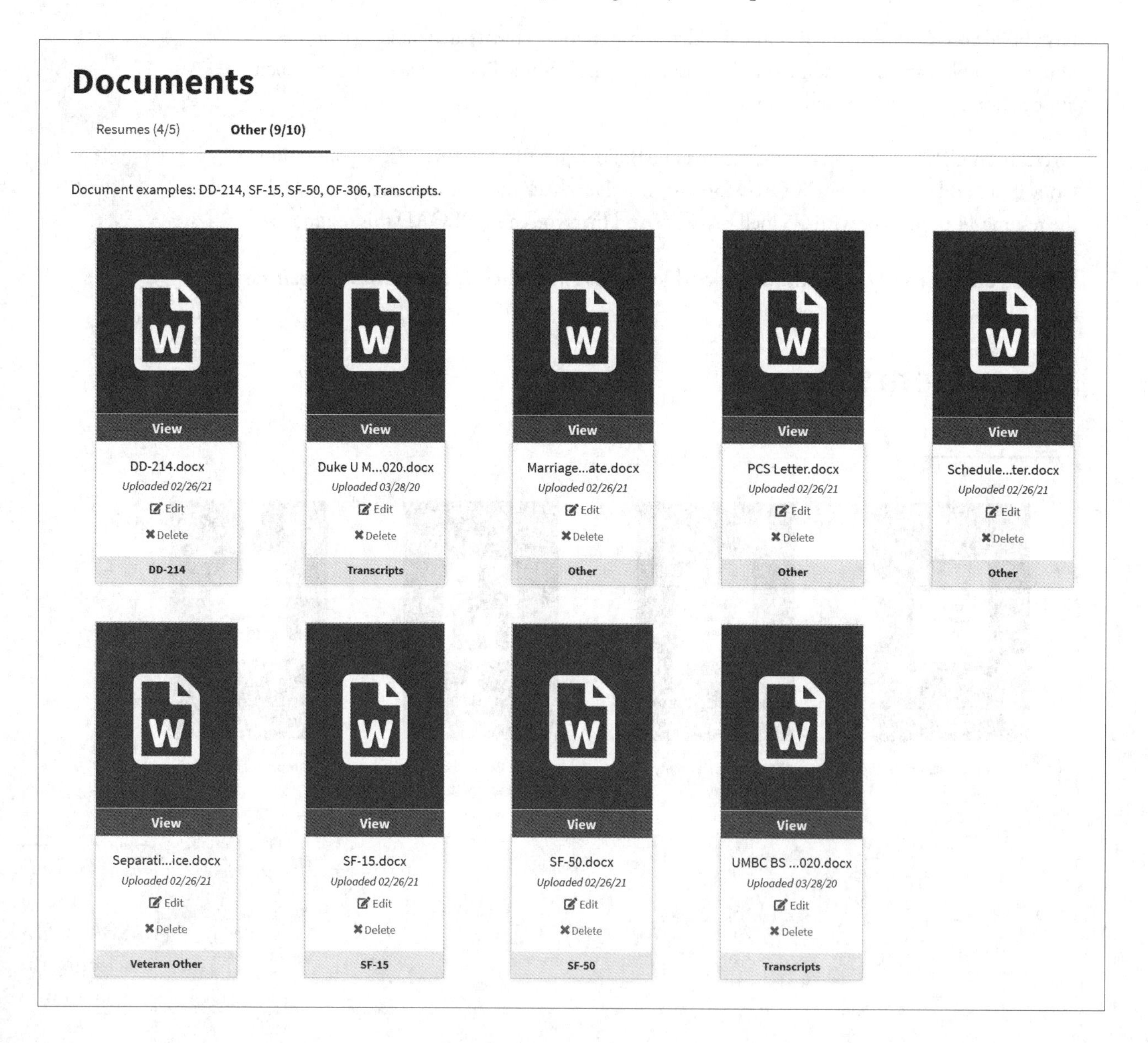

REQUIRED DOCUMENTS

You must include the required documents with your application, but this can often be difficult to determine. See the chart below for the most common documents required for special hiring paths. This chart is not guaranteed to be accurate for every announcement. You must read the *How To Apply* instructions in the USAJOBS announcement for the documents required for each application. Remember that it is safer to submit all documentation, even if not required, than to miss a required document.

Documents to Prove Eligibility for **Federal Hiring Programs**

Veterans' Preference

- DD-214 (honorable conditions discharge)

30% or More Disabled Veterans

- DD-214
- Disability letter from the Department of Veterans Affairs or Armed Service
- Standard Form (SF) 15

Spouse of an Active Duty Member of the Armed Forces

- Spouse's active military orders
- Marriage certificate
- Military Spouse PPP Self-Certification Checklist

Derived Preference for Spouse of a member of the Armed Forces who retired with a disability rating of 100 percent

Derived Preference for un-remarried widow or widower of a member of the Armed Forces killed while in active duty status

- SF-15
- DD-214(honorable conditions discharge)
- Death certificate and documentation identifying marital status at the time of death
- Disability letter from the Department of Veterans Affairs or Armed Service

Schedule A Disability

- Schedule A Letter signed by a licensed medical professional or vocational rehabilitation specialist to show proof of disability

Current or Former Federal Civilian Employee

- Most recent SF-50
- Most recent performance appraisal may be requested

Overseas Appropriated Fund Employee

- Most recent SF-50
- Most recent performance appraisal

Non-Competitive Eligibility (NCE) for Eligible Family Members and Employers (e.g., Family Liaison Office, US Dept. of State)

- First and last SF-50s for every federal position held
- Most recent signed performance review NCE Verification Letter

Displaced Employees

- Most recent SF-50
- Most recent performance appraisal
- Proof of eligibility letter from the Agency

PART TWO: APPLY FOR A FEDERAL JOB

Apply

This part of the application process is probably the most tricky and difficult to do. Correctly submitting the questionnaire (eligibility questions and job-related questions), documents, and resume are critical for your effort to get hired.

Who May Apply

Be sure to select the correct "Who May Apply" announcement for your situation. The first announcement is open to: Career transition (CTAP, ICTAP, RPL), Land & Base Management, Military Spouses, Other Hiring Authorities, Veterans and Competitive Service (Current Federal Employees). The second announcement is Open to the Public.

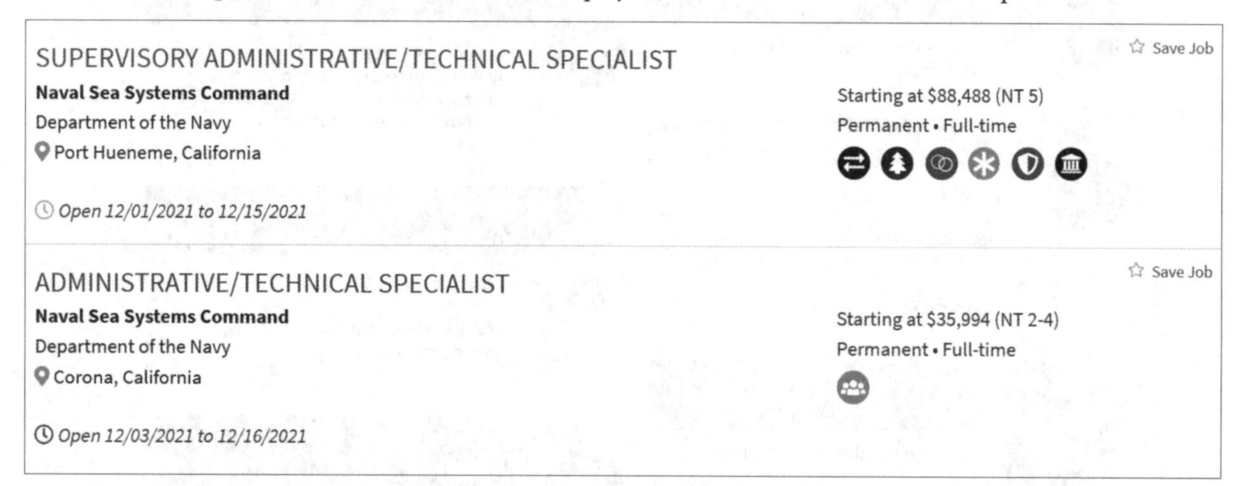

TOP TIPS: Select the right resume for a specific announcement.

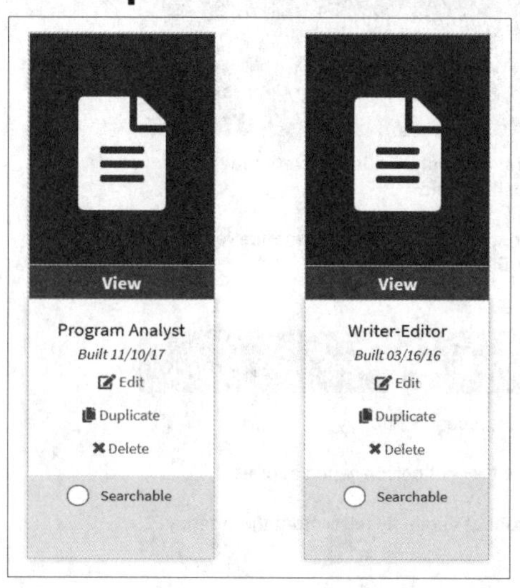

Select the right documents for the announcement.

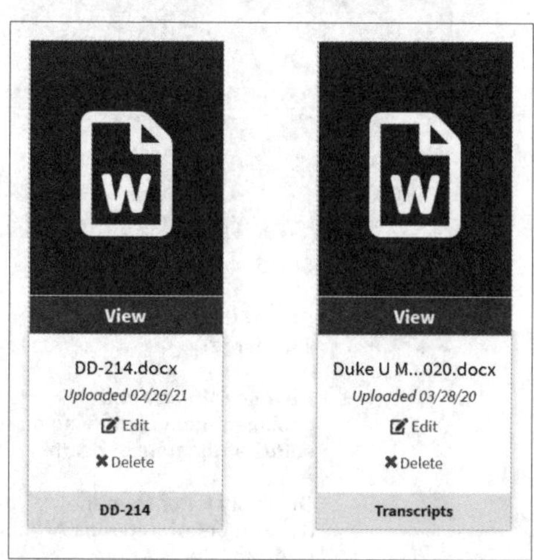

LOOK FOR JOB-RELATED QUESTIONNAIRE

After you complete your application in USAJOBS, you will be directed to complete it on the agency's application page.

Application Progress

Position Title	PARK RANGER (I)
Agency	National Park Service
Announcement Number	MW-1542-VOYA-22-11295894-DE
Open Period	Monday, December 6, 2021 to Friday, December 10, 2021

Application Package Status: Application Incomplete

Welcome KATHRYN TROUTMAN!

If you are not KATHRYN TROUTMAN please return to USAJOBS.

Please wait while we retrieve your information from USAJOBS.

Done! ✔

Thank you for your interest in the GS-7 PARK RANGER (I) position located in International Falls, MN.

Over the next few pages we are going to verify and collect pertinent information to help you complete your application for this position. You will be able to review and then submit your application to the National Park Service.

Important: ANSWER THE SELF-ASSESSMENT, JOB-RELATED QUESTIONS GIVING YOURSELF THE MOST CREDIT THAT YOU CAN. THIS IS A TEST! Your score will determine if you are Best Qualified for the position. The selection for E below gives you three options: You are an expert; you supervised this task; or you assist or train others in this task. If any of these apply to you, you can select E.

*2. Present informational talks, guided tours, briefings, and/or demonstrations to various audiences to inform or educate.

- ○ A. I have not had education, training, or experience in performing this task.
- ○ B. I have had education or training in how to perform this task, but have not yet performed it on the job.
- ○ C. I have performed this task on the job. My work on this task was monitored closely by a supervisor or senior employee to ensure compliance with proper procedures.
- ○ D. I have performed this task as a regular part of a job. I have performed it independently and normally without review by a supervisor or senior employee.
- ◉ E. I am considered an expert in performing this task. I have supervised performance of this task or am normally the person who is consulted by other workers to assist or train them in doing this task because of my expertise.

Document Upload

Use the dropdown to select your documents from your USAJOBS account. Make sure you NAME your documents correctly in USAJOBS for easy identification.

Note: Some documents may be designated as required **based on your responses to the questions in the "Eligibilities" section of this application. If you do not possess one or more of the required documents below, please review your answers to determine if your responses are accurate.**

Accepted Documents	Available Documents
Resume **(required)**	× Writer-Editor - View
Cover Letter	× Schedule A Letter - View
DD-214/ Statement of Service	× DD-214 - View
Disability Letter (Schedule A)	× Schedule A Letter - View
Disability Letter (VA)	
Other (1)	× UMBC BS IT Specialist 2020 - View

If the documents are not already in your USAJOBS account, you can upload them now. NAME the documents correctly for easy identification in this step.

Are you missing a document?

Upload

Make sure you hit the SUBMIT APPLICATION button after you see the three green checks.

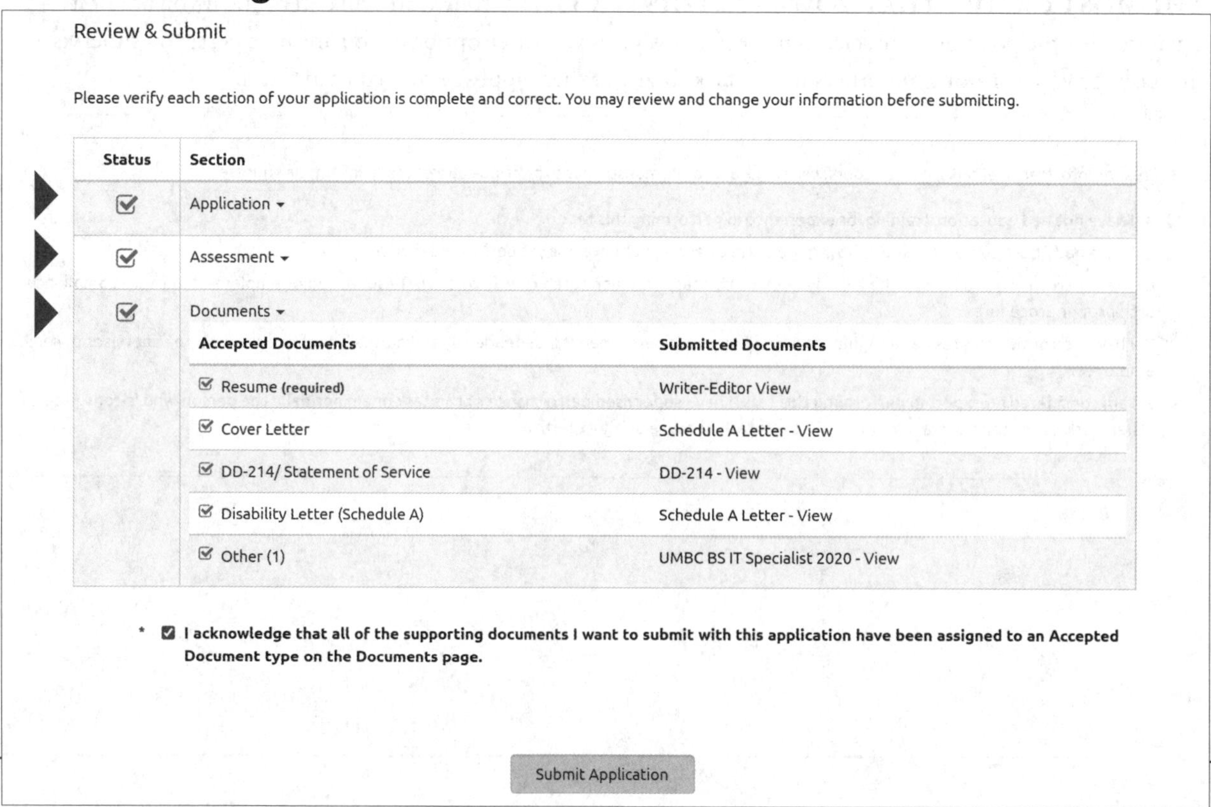
Review & Submit

Please verify each section of your application is complete and correct. You may review and change your information before submitting.

Status	Section
☑	Application ▾
☑	Assessment ▾
☑	Documents ▾

Accepted Documents	Submitted Documents
☑ Resume **(required)**	Writer-Editor View
☑ Cover Letter	Schedule A Letter - View
☑ DD-214/ Statement of Service	DD-214 - View
☑ Disability Letter (Schedule A)	Schedule A Letter - View
☑ Other (1)	UMBC BS IT Specialist 2020 - View

* ☑ **I acknowledge that all of the supporting documents I want to submit with this application have been assigned to an Accepted Document type on the Documents page.**

Submit Application

Processing Notification

After you hit submit, you will be redirected to a page that says that your application is being processed. The self-assessment questionnaire is rated immediately by the system. The Self-Assessment Rating will be given to the Human Resources Specialist within minutes online in the USA Staffing® system. You will receive an email from USA Staffing® to say that the resume was received and is being reviewed. You will receive additional emails with further status statements.

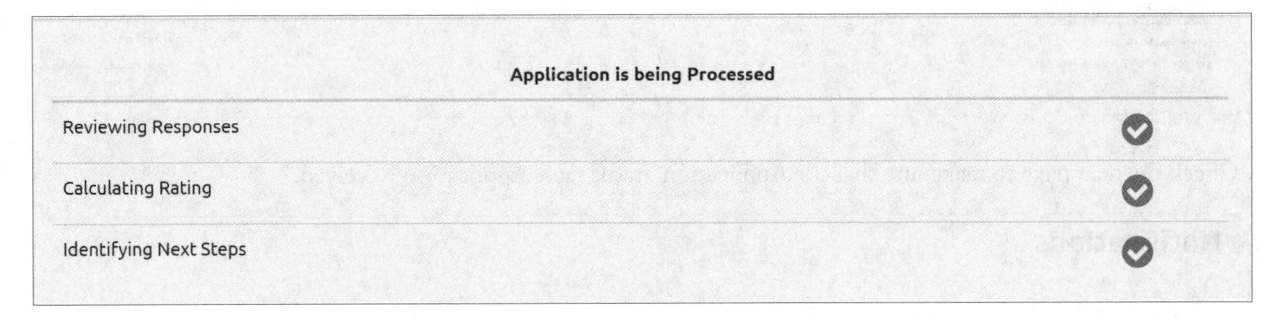

Successful Submission!

Make sure that you have completed the application and that you see a page resembling this one.

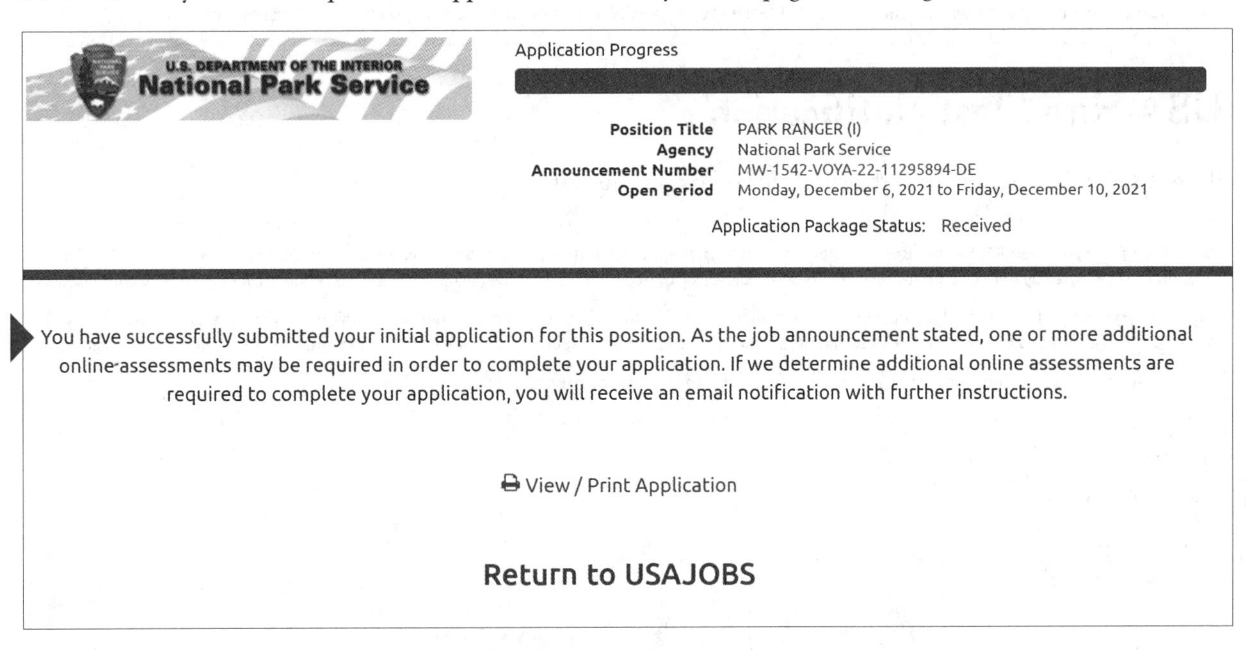

Make Sure Your Application Is Successfully Submitted (USAJOBS)

The Applications tab on the USAJOBS home page will contain a list of the jobs for which you have applied. You can click on the "Track this application" link for the application you just submitted.

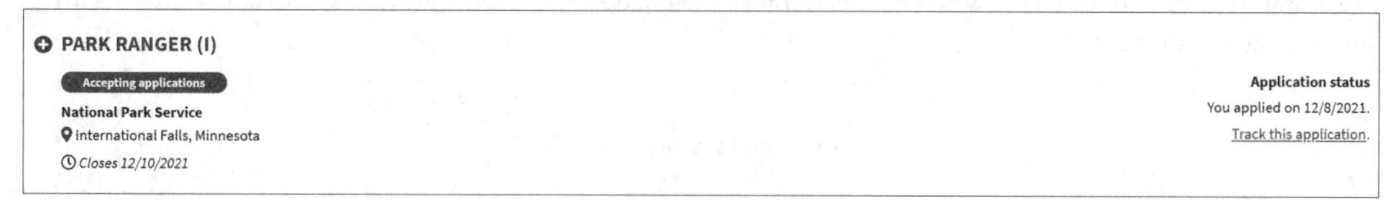

Check the next page to make sure that the Application Status says "Application Received."

Notifications

Date Sent	Email Subject
12/8/2021 3:59:50 PM	Action Needed for Announcement MW-1542-VOYA-22-11295894-DE Assessment Accommodation Request
12/8/2021 3:59:08 PM	Application for PARK RANGER (I), MW-1542-VOYA-22-11295894-DE was received.

Notification text may not be permanently retained. Please keep copies of all notifications sent to you for your personal records.

USA Hire℠ Test Notification

If a test is required, do not miss the email notice to take this test!

Step 1. Log into your USAJOBS application profile, and update your application to the Reasonable Accommodation Question from "Yes" to "No" or respond to this email by notifying us at USAHire_Accommodations@opm.gov to let us know you do not need to request a Reasonable Accommodation.

Next Steps: Once you complete this step, you should receive an email with a link to the unaccommodated version of the online assessment. You will need to complete this assessment by the date and time denoted in that email to submit a complete application and be considered for this position.

If you have any questions throughout this process, contact USAHire_Accommodations@opm.gov.

***

Sincerely,

USA Hire Program Office

STEP 9
TRACK YOUR APPLICATION & FOLLOW UP

Some Federal jobseekers will apply for years or for hundreds of times and do not know why they are not getting Referred. It's important to find out what happened with your applications. That way you can improve or change your application if you are frequently found to be Ineligible or Not Referred. You can follow up and troubleshoot your applications to improve your chances of getting REFERRED, INTERVIEWED, and SELECTED.

Download All Applications

If you are applying to numerous announcements, it can be helpful to have a spreadsheet of your applications. Click on EXPORT APPLICATIONS to download the information for all of the applications that you submitted through USAJOBS.

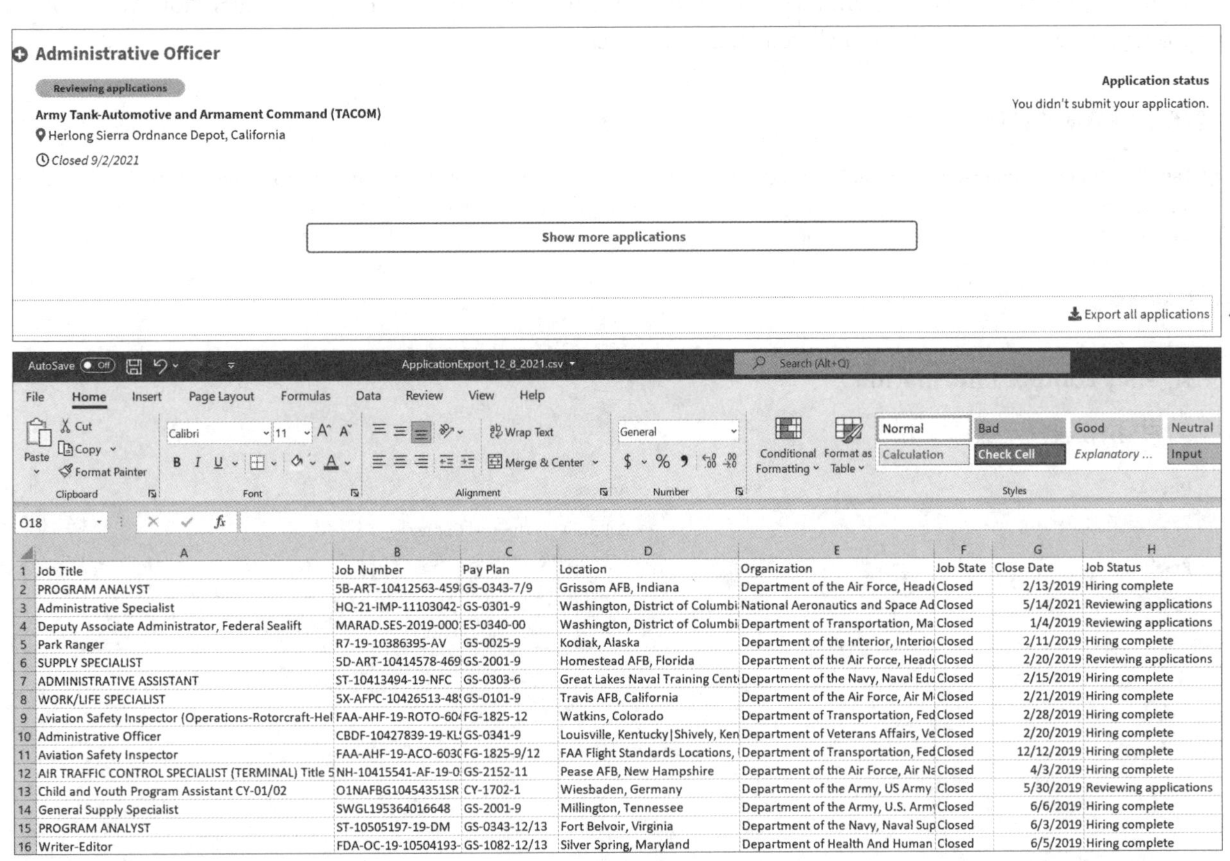

	A	B	C	D	E	F	G	H
1	Job Title	Job Number	Pay Plan	Location	Organization	Job State	Close Date	Job Status
2	PROGRAM ANALYST	5B-ART-10412563-459	GS-0343-7/9	Grissom AFB, Indiana	Department of the Air Force, Head	Closed	2/13/2019	Hiring complete
3	Administrative Specialist	HQ-21-IMP-11103042-	GS-0301-9	Washington, District of Columbi	National Aeronautics and Space Ad	Closed	5/14/2021	Reviewing applications
4	Deputy Associate Administrator, Federal Sealift	MARAD.SES-2019-000	ES-0340-00	Washington, District of Columbi	Department of Transportation, Ma	Closed	1/4/2019	Reviewing applications
5	Park Ranger	R7-19-10386395-AV	GS-0025-9	Kodiak, Alaska	Department of the Interior, Interio	Closed	2/11/2019	Hiring complete
6	SUPPLY SPECIALIST	5D-ART-10414578-469	GS-2001-9	Homestead AFB, Florida	Department of the Air Force, Head	Closed	2/20/2019	Reviewing applications
7	ADMINISTRATIVE ASSISTANT	ST-10413494-19-NFC	GS-0303-6	Great Lakes Naval Training Cent	Department of the Navy, Naval Edu	Closed	2/15/2019	Hiring complete
8	WORK/LIFE SPECIALIST	5X-AFPC-10426513-48	GS-0101-9	Travis AFB, California	Department of the Air Force, Air M	Closed	2/21/2019	Hiring complete
9	Aviation Safety Inspector (Operations-Rotorcraft-Hel	FAA-AHF-19-ROTO-60	FG-1825-12	Watkins, Colorado	Department of Transportation, Fed	Closed	2/28/2019	Hiring complete
10	Administrative Officer	CBDF-10427839-19-KL	GS-0341-9	Louisville, Kentucky|Shively, Ken	Department of Veterans Affairs, Ve	Closed	2/20/2019	Hiring complete
11	Aviation Safety Inspector	FAA-AHF-19-ACO-603	FG-1825-9/12	FAA Flight Standards Locations,	Department of Transportation, Fed	Closed	12/12/2019	Hiring complete
12	AIR TRAFFIC CONTROL SPECIALIST (TERMINAL) Title 5	NH-10415541-AF-19-0	GS-2152-11	Pease AFB, New Hampshire	Department of the Air Force, Air Na	Closed	4/3/2019	Hiring complete
13	Child and Youth Program Assistant CY-01/02	O1NAFBG10454351SR	CY-1702-1	Wiesbaden, Germany	Department of the Army, US Army	Closed	5/30/2019	Reviewing applications
14	General Supply Specialist	SWGL195364016648	GS-2001-9	Millington, Tennessee	Department of the Army, U.S. Arm	Closed	6/6/2019	Hiring complete
15	PROGRAM ANALYST	ST-10505197-19-DM	GS-0343-12/13	Fort Belvoir, Virginia	Department of the Navy, Naval Sup	Closed	6/3/2019	Hiring complete
16	Writer-Editor	FDA-OC-19-10504193-	GS-1082-12/13	Silver Spring, Maryland	Department of Health And Human	Closed	6/5/2019	Hiring complete

APPLICATION RESULTS: CHECK YOUR EMAILS

You will receive the results of your applications by email from **USAStaffingOffice@opm.gov**.

These responses indicate that you were not found to be Best Qualified or Referred:

- ✖ NOT REFERRED
- ✖ INELIGIBLE
- ✖ DO NOT MEET THE AREAS OF CONSIDERATION REQUIREMENTS
- ✖ DO NOT POSSESS THE SPECIALIZED EXPERIENCE
- ✖ INELIGIBLE BASED ON SELF-RATINGS
- ✖ DO NOT MEET TRAINING REQUIREMENTS
- ✖ DOCUMENTATION YOU PROVIDED FAILED TO SHOW THE ELIGIBILITY REQUIREMENTS

Follow Up and Follow Through Are Key!

Follow up with the HR person who is listed on the announcement to find out why you received this rating. It is better to email your request. Make the Subject line of the email: Request Explanation, Your name, announcement number, title of the position. Ask why you are ineligible or not referred. It's important to find out what is wrong with your applications if you are continually receiving Ineligible or Out of the Area of Consideration. Work to improve your resume and application based on this feedback.

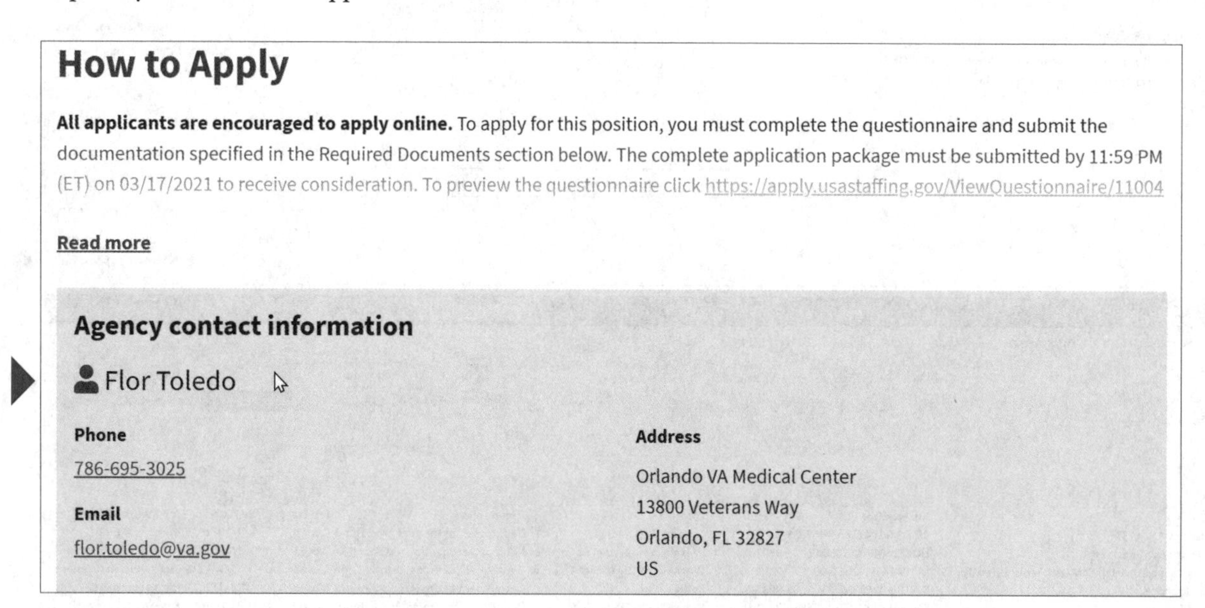

SAMPLE RESULTS EMAILS

RESULTS: INELIGIBLE, NOT REFERRED, OR NOT SELECTED

Position Title: **Office Automation Assistant**

You were found:
Ineligible for the following position or positions:

- ✖ GS-0326-5; You were **not considered** because you do not meet the Area of Consideration requirements as specified in the announcement.

The following is your referral status for the position or positions to which you applied:

- ✖ You have **not been referred** to the hiring manager for position GS-0326-5 in Ventura, California.

Position Title: **Technical Training Program Assistant**
Pay Plan - Series - Grade: GS-0303-7

Your rating is: **Ineligible** for the following position or positions:

- ✖ GS-0303-7; You are ineligible because you do not possess the specialized experience required for this position.

The following is your referral status for the position or positions to which you applied:

- ✖ You have **not been referred** to the hiring manager for position GS-0303-7 in Washington, District of Columbia.

SAMPLE RESULTS EMAILS (CONT)

This is a record of the results and referral status for the position of **Student Trainee** (Business & Industry) with Departmental Administration—ONE USDA as detailed in Announcement ONEUSDA-10643368-20-NS.

Ineligible for the following position or positions:

✖ GS-1199-5; You are ineligible because you **failed to meet the training/education** qualification requirements for this series/specialty/grade combination.

✖ GS-1199-4; You were not considered for this position because your **application does not show that you meet the eligibility requirements for the Pathways Internship Program** as specified in the vacancy announcement.

Subject: Notice of Results and Referral for **Public Affairs Specialist**, GS-1035-12/13, 20-R6-10724636-G-VH.

Ineligible for the following position or positions:

✖ GS-1035-13; You were not considered for this position because the documentation you provided **failed to support the eligibility** you selected at the time of application.

The following is your referral status for the position or positions to which you applied:

✖ You have **not been referred** to the hiring manager for position GS-1035-13 in Portland, Oregon.

This is a record of the selection decision for the position of **Park Manager** (Superintendent) at National Capital Area Office as detailed in Announcement NC-1616-NCRO-20-10880432-ST.

We regret to inform you that you were **not selected** for the position of:

✖ GS-0025-13 in Frederick, Maryland

RESULTS: REFERRED TO THE SUPERVISOR (Great News!)

Vacancy Identification Number: 10863661
Position Title: **Victim Advocate** (Sexual Harassment/Assault Response & Prevention)
Series and Grade: 0101-9
Hiring Office: EV-APF-W0AKAA US ARMY ALASKA, HQ

Your rating is:
Eligible for the following position or positions:

- GS-0101-9; You are tentatively eligible for this series/grade combination based on your self-rating of your qualifications.

The following is your referral status for the position or positions to which you applied:

- You **have been referred** to the hiring manager for position GS-0101-9 in Fort Richardson, Alaska.

Subject: Notice of Referral for **Deputy District Director**, 20-085-DB | 10702446

The following is your referral status for the position or positions to which you applied:

- You **have been referred** to the hiring manager for position GS-0340-14 in Columbus, OH.

RESULTS: HIRED (The Best News of All!)

SELECTED

Congratulations on your tentative offer of employment with the U.S. Small Business Administration, Office of Disaster Assistance, Processing and Disbursement Center - PDC, Duty Station is determined by your official residence.

Appointment Type: Schedule A-(Temporary Employment)
Attorney Advisor (Gen)
GS-0905-11-1 which equates to $30.67 an hour on the Rest of United States (RUS) locality pay scale.

Depending on your official residence address, you may make more, but you will not make less than the amount quoted above. You may find the locality pay scale associated with your residence address at this web site: https://www.opm.gov/policy-data-oversight/pay-leave/salaries-wages/2020/general-schedule/

No Relocation Expenses will be paid.

Your initial appointment is for a period of greater than 90 days and therefore allows limited benefits: Federal Employee Health Benefits (FEHB), sick and annual leave accrual.

(Continued on next page)

SAMPLE RESULTS EMAILS (CONT)

This offer is contingent upon the needs of the Office of Disaster Assistance (ODA) in response to a disaster. Please be aware that work hours and days may vary in support of the disaster. ODA employees should expect to work up to seven (7) days per week, possibly 10-12 hours each day. Overtime is mandatory.

This position is remote, you will telework from your residence. As a condition of employment, you must have high-speed internet and a telephone, either cellular or landline. Your high-speed internet cannot be through your cellular phone.

CONGRATULATIONS - OFFER LETTER!

From: usastaffingoffice@opm.gov

Sent: Wednesday, January 13, 2021 1:53 PM

Subject: Tentative Job Offer - Employment Requirements - Benjamin Matwey / Joint Base Anacostia-Bolling, District of Columbia - AF-20NOV9LHILLK00112107

Dear ---- ,

Congratulations! You have been **tentatively selected for the position of PUBLIC AFFAIRS SPECIALIST, GS- 1035-11** located at Joint Base Anacostia-Bolling, District of Columbia. **Starting salary is GS-11, Step 06** at $84,879 Per Year. This employment offer is contingent upon receiving notice of acceptance of this tentative offer within two (2) business days of receipt of this offer. If you do not respond to acknowledge acceptance or declination by 15 Jan 2021, this job offer will be withdrawn.

First Step - You must accept this tentative job offer AND activate your New Hire record using the link below. The link will take you to the offer acceptance page. After submitting your acceptance, you will be directed to login.gov where you will utilize your USAJOBS account to login to New Hire to activate your New Hire record and begin the onboarding process. Your record is activated after successful login. You can start the onboarding process after successfully logging in, or you can return at a later time. You must use the tentative offer link below to accept this job offer and activate your New Hire record. Merely accessing your USAJOBS account will not present the New Hire welcome page. Click (or copy/paste) the following link to accept this tentative job offer AND activate your New Hire record:

https://onboard.usastaffing.gov/?selectee=a1055787-1515-49a3-98b1-3945529471af&type=tentative

TIME TO NEGOTIATE! If you are a first-time Federal hire, you might be able to negotiate your step, tuition reimbursement, or other benefits. See page 139 for details!

A TURNAROUND STORY FROM INELIGIBLE TO SELECTED BY WRITING TO HUMAN RESOURCES

RESULTS: INELIGIBLE – THEN SELECTED AND NEGOTIATED HIGH STEP

FEDERAL AGENCY INELIGIBLE EMAIL
Date: 6/9/2020 12:58:15 PM
From: USA Staffing
Subject: Application Status - MDA-20-DH-10815114

Matthew,

This refers to the application you recently submitted to this office for the position: GENERAL ENGINEER NH-0801-4

We have completed the review of your application for this position. Your application will receive no further consideration, for the following reason:

Ineligible for the following position or positions:
* NH-0801-4; You are ineligible because you do not possess the specialized experience required for this position. Thank you for your interest.

APPLICANT REQUEST FOR RECONSIDERATION

From: Matt
Sent: Wednesday, June 10, 2020 8:53 AM
To: Federal Human Resources
Subject: Inquiry Please

Dear Human Resources Staffing,

Could you please allow me to better understand why I was not referred for the position in Announcement 1234567.
I have ten plus years on the Missile Program inclusive of six years as a Quality Engineer on complicated weapon systems.
Yet, the response I received was I have no specialized experience for the position? Could someone please explain that to me?

V/R, Matt

AGENCY HUMAN RESOURCES RESPONSE

From: Federal Human Resources
Sent: Friday, June 12, 2020 2:49 PM
To: Matt
Subject: RE: Inquiry Please

Good Afternoon, The notes have that you lack specialized experience in applying quality, safety, ad mission assurance techniques on weapon system components. Experience with all aspects of Engineering technical consulting involved with complex weapon systems, to include risk management. Experience in the application of military, industry, and commercial quality and safety standards is recommended along with the ability to apply that knowledge to determine technical suitability of weapon system design. Experience with prohibited and restricted materials to include identifying proper mitigations and risk evaluation criteria for various restricted parts and materials with above average risk for weapons system usage. Experience contributing to failure review boards, engineering reviews, technical interchange meetings, monitor testing and qualification activities.

Thank you for your interest, Hiring Team

APPLICANT REQUEST FOR RECONSIDERATION AGAIN

From: Matthew C CIV
Sent: Friday, June 12, 2020 2:57 PM
To: Human Resources Recruiter
Subject: RE: Inquiry Please

Dear Hiring Team,

I totally disagree and each aspect of the below ksa's have been answered and documented in my resume, both as Quality Assurance Engineer, as a NAVY PMO Resident and as today's section lead. I believe this is in error and I am challenging this rating, requesting reconsideration. V/R, Matt

---

FINAL RESULTS: SELECTED – NEGOTIATED HIGH STEP! SUCCESS!

Subject: Accepted Counter Offer

Morning Kathryn, Negotiations went back and forth a bit, but I finally settled on 153,4+ K and accepted. All is good, awaiting start date. Thank you again for all the help!

V/R, Matt

STEP 10
INTERVIEW & NEGOTIATE

WORKSHEET: INTERVIEW PREPARATION

Start preparing for the interview: answer these questions.

Tell Me About Yourself:
Write a short introduction you could use in an interview. It should include information relevant to the position.

Significant Accomplishment:
Write one significant accomplishment that you will describe in an interview.

Best Competencies:
Make a list of your best competencies. See Step 5 for info on competencies.

Most Valuable Skills:
Make a list of your best skills that would be most valued by an employer.

Present your best competencies with a great story or example that demonstrates your real behavior. Use the space below to practice using the CCAR method in answering this question prompt.

Can you give me an example of a problem at work or school that you solved?

CONTEXT

CHALLENGE

ACTION

RESULTS

THE BEHAVIOR-BASED INTERVIEW IS A TEST

The Federal job interview is a test. You will be scored.

The Federal interview format is called the **behavior-based interview**. This means that they will ask you open-ended questions about your experiences that might be related to the position.

Be prepared to answer 7 to 10 questions that will be situational or experience-based. The best answers will be examples that show you already demonstrated the skill or ability in the past. You will want to prepare answers that include accomplishments in the CCAR format (see Step 7 and previous page). For example, tell how you led a team, provided training for others, or managed a project.

So, for instance, for the IT Specialist position at West Point, the questions could be:

Information Technology Specialist (Customer Support)

DEPARTMENT OF THE ARMY

U.S. Military Academy, Office of the Dean, Department of Physics

Basic Requirement for IT Specialist, GS-07 grade level:
Specialized and Other Experience - One year of specialized experience which includes:
1) Provide basic software training for users; **Can you tell me about a time when you provided basic training for users of a software package?**
2) Utilize basic data processing methods in support of the organization's mission; **Can you tell me about a time when you utilized data processing for your courses or a project? What was the program and what was your project?**
3) Utilize computer software programs or computer processing programs to prepare reports; **Can you tell me about a report you produced, the software you used and the final output?**
4) Develop virtual learning technology and curriculum for Physics courses. **Can you tell me about a virtual learning project and the curriculum you developed or presented in the virtual learning?**

TYPICAL BEHAVIOR-BASED INTERVIEW QUESTIONS

Typical interview questions will be:

Job-Related
Open-Ended
Behavior-Based
Skill- and Competency-Based

Competency-Based Sample Interview Questions

Often, an interviewer will ask questions that directly relate to a competency required for the position. Here are some examples.

- **Attention to Detail:** Describe a project you were working on that required attention to detail.
- **Communication:** Describe a time when you had to communicate under difficult circumstances.
- **Conflict Management:** Describe a situation where you found yourself working with someone who didn't like you. How did you handle it?
- **Continuous Learning:** Describe a time when you recognized a problem as an opportunity.
- **Customer Service:** Describe a situation in which you demonstrated an effective customer service skill.
- **Decisiveness:** Tell me about a time when you had to stand up for a decision you made even though it made you unpopular.
- **Leadership:** Describe a time when you demonstrated leadership.
- **Planning, Organizing, Goal-Setting:** Describe a time when you had to complete multiple tasks. What method did you use to manage your time?
- **Presentation:** Tell me about a time when you developed a lesson, training, or briefing and presented it to a group.
- **Problem Solving:** Describe a time when you analyzed data to determine multiple solutions to a problem. What steps did you take?
- **Team Work:** Describe a time when you had to deal with a team member who was not pulling his/her weight.

STEP 10

INTERVIEW TIPS

Steps to prepare and practice

1. Find the job announcement for the interview.

2. Find the SPECIALIZED EXPERIENCE PARAGRAPH to create possible questions for the interview.

3. Write the answers to these questions on paper. For instance, you can give an example of a time when you "provide basic training for users of a software package."

4. Write five projects / or assignment "stories" to prepare. Use the CCAR Accomplishment Builder to write your five examples of your past experience.

   See Builder at:
   https://resume-place.com/resources/ccar-accomplishment-builder/

5. Practice speaking your stories with your cell phone or with someone who will listen and give you feedback, such as a career counselor or a friend.

Know the Background
Know the vacancy announcement, agency mission, and office function. Read your resume and KSAs out loud and with enthusiasm.

Do Your Research
Go online to research the agency, department, and position. Read press releases about the organization. Search for recent news about the agency.

Confidence, Knowledge, and Skills
In order to "sell yourself," you need to believe in your abilities. It is not bragging to share what you have accomplished. Don't forget or be afraid to use "I"! Use eye contact.

Types of Interviews
You may be asked to conduct a telephone, virtual platform, or in-person interview; it may be with an individual or with a panel or group.

FINALLY: PREPARATION AND PRACTICE ARE KEY TO PASSING THE TELEPHONE, VIRTUAL PLATFORM, OR IN-PERSON INTERVIEW.

NEGOTIATING YOUR JOB OFFER

CONGRATULATIONS—YOU RECEIVED YOUR JOB OFFER!

Sample job offer

> *Congratulations! You have been tentatively selected for a position as a Social Worker GS-0185-11 located at Fort Hood, TX.*
>
> *The starting salary for this position is set at GS-0185-11 (Step 1, $59,246) per annum, which includes a locality payment of 14.35%.*

Now what? You can now negotiate the offer with a Superior Qualifications Justification Narrative!

> **Superior Qualifications Determination**
>
> An agency may determine that a candidate has superior qualifications based on—
>
> - the level, type, or quality of the candidate's skills or competencies demonstrated or obtained through experience and/or education;
> - the quality of the candidate's accomplishments compared to others in the field; or
> - other factors that support a superior qualifications determination.
>
> The candidate's skills, competencies, experience, education, and/or accomplishments must be relevant to the requirements of the position to be filled. These qualities must be significantly higher than that needed to be minimally qualified for the position and/or be of a more specialized quality compared to other candidates.

https://www.opm.gov/policy-data-oversight/pay-leave/pay-administration/fact-sheets/superior-qualifications-and-special-needs-pay-setting-authority/

Key negotiation points:

- Request a day or two to evaluate and respond to the offer.
- The job offer will not be withdrawn in response to your negotiation request.
- Prepare a written statement to make your request and explain your justification. Send this statement to the HR Specialist, who will present the document to the hiring manager for consideration if needed.
- Your chances of success with negotiation will depend on many variables, such as your qualifications, the organization budget, and the importance of the position to the organization mission.
- In some situations, if you reject the job offer, the agency will need to restart the hiring process again to fill the position. At other times, there will be a list of candidates ranked in order for hiring, and the next applicant will be offered the position if you reject it.

What can you negotiate?

- Salary
- Annual leave
- Recruitment incentive
- Telework
- Tuition reimbursement
- Reasonable accommodations
- Relocation expenses
- Commuter transit subsidy

NEGOTIATING YOUR JOB OFFER

Salary

You must accept the grade level that was advertised in the announcement, but you can negotiate your step within the grade level, all the way up to Step 10. To negotiate a higher grade, write a Superior Qualifications letter or memo to explain why your qualifications are significantly higher than what is required for the position or others who have applied. You can include salary information if it is greater than their offer.

Annual Leave

Did you know? Your non-federal work experience may also be considered towards the calculation of your annual leave if it will serve to achieve an agency mission or performance goal.

More details: *https://www.opm.gov/policy-data-oversight/pay-leave/*

Recruitment Incentive

Some agencies may have a plan in place to pay a recruitment incentive if the position is difficult to fill.

https://www.opm.gov/policy-data-oversight/pay-leave/recruitment-relocation-retention-incentives/fact-sheets/recruitment-incentives/

Telework

You can ask if your position qualifies for part-time telecommuting.

www.telework.gov/guidance-legislation/telework-guidance/recruitment-retention/

Tuition Reimbursement

If you or your children have Federal student loans, you can ask for the organization to assist with your student loan repayment before you accept the position.

https://www.opm.gov/policy-data-oversight/pay-leave/student-loan-repayment/

Reasonable Accommodations

If you are a Schedule A applicant, you can ask for reasonable accommodations to help you perform your job, such as modifications to facilities for accessibility, modification of work schedule or location, and/or equipment.

www.telework.gov/guidance-legislation/telework-guidance/reasonable-accommodations/

Relocation Expenses

Many vacancy announcements will state that moving expenses will not be reimbursed. However, if you have leverage in the negotiation process, and you do have to move, you could ask for some compensation toward your moving expenses.

The results of offer negotiation vary widely and depend on the agency, the budget, your qualifications, your narrative request, and the supervisor's decision. What we tell people is that it will not hurt you to ask.

Possible Responses from HR

- If your request is accepted, congratulations on your new position!
- If your request is partially accepted and a revised offer is extended, you can accept or reject that offer, or present a counteroffer.
- When the hiring agency is no longer willing to make any more adjustments to the offer, then you will need to decide whether or not to accept the position.

SAMPLE SUPERIOR QUALIFICATIONS LETTER

To: John Mercens, Human Resources, Center for Disease Control and Prevention
From: Carlisle Amhearst
Subject: Superior Qualifications Statement for Training Specialist (GS-12)
Date: February 2, 20xx

Thank you for the offer of employment for the Training Specialist position with the Center for Disease Control and Prevention's Office of Public Health Preparedness and Response. I look forward to having the opportunity to contribute to the development and implementation of training to support the mission of the Division of State and Local Readiness.

At this time, I would like to request that based upon superior qualifications, I receive an increase to GS-12 Step 4 or a sign-on bonus in the amount of 25% of my starting pay.

Through my education and work experience, I have had the opportunity to demonstrate superior qualifications in the following ways:

1. I have planned, directed, and taught a variety of public health preparedness and emergency response courses over the past five years for the Maryland Fire and Rescue Institute and the past three years for Howard Community College, totaling to over 25 courses taught.

2. I have prepared a wide array of teaching materials for and taught over 30 public health science courses over the past nine years at the University of Maryland.

3. My doctoral dissertation research has directly prepared me to focus on assessment and learning outcomes.

4. My educational background includes doctoral training in Biomedical Sciences Education, a Masters degree in Infectious Disease Education, and a Bachelors degree in Cell and Molecular Biology and Genetics.

5. I have served on the front lines in emergency response for the past fifteen years as an Emergency Medical Technician and Firefighter with the Laurel and Beltsville Volunteer Fire Departments in Prince George's County, Maryland, just outside of Washington, DC.

I sincerely appreciate your consideration of this request, and I look forward to beginning a rewarding career with the Centers for Disease Control and Prevention and making an impact within the Office of Public Health Preparedness and Response.

SAMPLE SUPER QUALIFICATIONS LETTER RECENT GRADUATE

BRIAN FOX
Address
Phone / Email
Date

Deputy Chief of Staff for Information Technology (DCSIT),
Cybersecurity (CS)
Defense Language Institute Foreign Language Center (DLIFLC),
Presidio of Monterey. California

Dear Human Resources Specialist,

I am grateful for this offer of a permanent appointment at the Defense Language Institute for a IT Specialist, (INFOSEC), (GS7 / Step 3). I highly value the opportunity to contribute daily to the development and implementation of training to support the mission of the Defense Language Institute.

Based upon my Superior Qualifications, I would like to request:

- Recruitment Incentive Bonus in the amount of 25% of my starting pay and Step 4 for the GS 7.
- Tuition Reimbursement for Federal Student Loans
- Telecommute work
- Relocation cost assistance for moving from Maryland to California

Through my current positions and educational training, I've had the opportunity to demonstrate Superior Qualifications in the following ways:

1. As an ORISE fellow at the Food and Drug Administration (FDA), Office of Translational Sciences (OTS), I contributed datamining, health information technology transfer and knowledge management for initiatives of the Center for Drug Evaluation and Research (CDER).
2. I have completed the requirements for a Statistics minor with coursework in Probability & Statistics for Science and Engineering, Time Series Data Analysis, Introduction to Probability Theory, and Applied Statistics.
3. I have participated in the weekly UMBC Cyber Dogs non-credit program since Fall 2019, which provides hands-on experience with a broad range of cyber security applications and tools. Some projects I have completed which are relevant to the job description of a DNEA include:
   d. Configuring Linux ip tables to implement state checks, HTTP/HTTPS, incoming/outgoing SSH, mailing protocols, and name resolution
   e. Exploring the iptables firewall configuration utility in Linux, including forwarding with pre/post routing, and writing policy chains

I look forward to beginning a rewarding career with the NSA and I am hopeful that you are able to respond favorably to this request to facilitate resources in support of my permanent appointment.

Thank you again.

Sincerely,

Brian Fox

FEDERAL CAREER CERTIFICATION AND LICENSING

RESUME PLACE

BUILDING CAREERS IN THE US GOVERNMENT

March 11, 2020 – Loyola College, Columbia, MD – our last CFJST / CFCC Live Class!

Certified Federal Job Search Trainer / Certified Federal Career Coach Program, 8 weeks, 90 min webinars. **The ground-breaking Ten Steps to a Federal Job® Certification Program** is the US Government Human Resources' most-respected and most-recognized Federal job search training and career coaching credential. Successfully complete the program and you will earn TWO certifications:

- **Certified Federal Job Search Trainer® (CFJST)**
- **Certified Federal Career Coach® (CFCC)**

You'll also receive your Exclusive Instructor's License for the Ten Steps® curriculum.

- **Ten Steps to a Federal Job®**
- **The Stars Are Lined Up for Military Spouses® on USAJOBS –** ***Winner of Two Book Awards***
- **Writing Your First Resume®**
- **Ten Steps to a Pathways Internship for Students and Recent Grads©**

Dates, Rates, and Program Information

https://resume-place.com/get-certified/ten-steps-trainer-certification/

ABOUT THE AUTHOR, KATHRYN TROUTMAN

1. Founder, President, and Manager of The Resume Place®, the first Federal job search consulting and Federal resume writing service in the world, and the producer of www.resume-place.com, the first website devoted to Federal resume writing.

2. Pioneer designer of the Federal resume format in 1995 with the publication of the leading resource for Federal human resources and jobseekers worldwide—the *Federal Resume Guidebook*—now in its seventh edition and the #2 resume book on the internet.

3. Developer of the Certified Federal Job Search Trainer®/Certified Federal Career Coach® train-the-trainer program in 2002. Licensing Ten Steps to a Federal Job®, a curriculum and turnkey training program taught by more than 5,000 Certified Federal Job Search Trainers® (CFJST) around the world. Recommended by military services for transition and employment readiness counselors around the world.

RESUME PLACE

BUILDING CAREERS IN THE US GOVERNMENT